TURNING WATER INTO BUTTER

A SPIRITUAL MEMOIR BY SAMMY ORELIEN

Hope this inspires you.

♡

Sammy

TURNING WATER INTO BUTTER

LIVING THE POWER WITHIN

A SPIRITUAL MEMOIR BY SAMMY ORELIEN

Turning Water into Butter: Living the Power Within
Copyright © 2024 by Dr. Jean-Guilmond Orelien
All rights reserved.

Published by
Universalis Publishing
Cheshire, Massachusetts

Cover design by Suzanne Nessi
Book design by: Sue Balcer

ISBN ebook: 979-8-9920649-0-2
ISBN paperback: 979-8-9920649-3-3
ISBN Hardback: 979-8-9920649-1-9

I dedicate this book to my mother, Marie Liliane Orelien, and to the generations before her—represented by my maternal grandmother, Gran Thérèse—who have planted the seeds of ultimate alchemy by showing us how to turn water into butter.

Table of Contents

Acknowledgments

A book is an endeavor that extends beyond its writer. I'm grateful to the many friends and consultants who reviewed earlier versions of this manuscript, providing guidance and feedback that shaped it into the final product. This book would not be what it is without their invaluable input.

Living with an intimate partner while writing a book inevitably affects them, whether they contribute to it directly or not. Writing takes time away from "us time" together, and when a partner reads and reviews multiple versions, that contribution deserves recognition. My beloved soulmate, Jala, has spent hours reviewing drafts, offering insightful feedback, and enhancing ideas. Although this is a memoir and I am the one who experienced these events, the interpretation and lessons drawn from them are shaped in the present, with Jala as a sounding board, helping me reframe these moments.

Among the many consultants who supported this project, two deserve special mention. Joseph Marcello reviewed early drafts, acting as a sounding board and offering perspectives. His most important contribution, though, was the inspiration to live the book's message fully and share it with others. Sue Balcer handled the typesetting and design of the book. I am grateful for her patience and attention to detail in accommodating last-minute changes.

Several individuals gave detailed reviews and candid feedback that significantly enriched the manuscript. I thank Patrick Moynahan and my cousins, Flaurie Martin, and Josette Teneus, for their thorough input.

Lastly, I want to acknowledge those who played a critical role in bringing this book to life. Jane Shealy first planted the idea of writing a book. Antonio Albano and Barney Brown, friends, and mentors since 2020, inspired reflections on love through our conversations and their beautiful property. Bill Buxton, my former executive coach for more than ten years, was instrumental in my spiritual journey, introducing me to resources such as the Landmark Forum, Dorrier Underwood, and the teachings of Father Richard Rohr. Jane Smith from Dorrier Underwood, a coach and mentor for many years, offered wisdom beyond words.

I once heard of an artist who never signed his paintings, explaining that inspiration came from everyone he met and didn't know how to credit them all. To everyone who has, at some point, held space for me, shared a smile, or offered a word of encouragement—thank you for your indirect contribution to this book. To my siblings—Gladys, Euphonia, Volande, Cardone, Luna, Jonas, Williams, Wilson, Stanley, Ruth, Chango, Alex and Joanne—thank you for putting up with me as the "special one". I honor the memories of Gilberte, Sperkland, and Camille who are no longer with us. To my cousins, I am grateful that so many of you are like brothers and sisters. Unfortunately, it would not be fair to the readers of this book to list each one of you. To my nephews, nieces, former and current colleagues, clients, collaborators, and friends—thank you for every piece you have contributed to the puzzle that is my life.

In the spirit of gratitude, I end this section with a heartfelt acknowledgment of Valery, who was my best friend and life co-pi-lot for over 25 years. To my children, Katina, Vladimir, Vijay, and Valexa, who hold a special place in my heart, this book is, in many ways, inspired by the unconditional love I have for you.

Foreword

Writing a book is an undertaking that requires deep reflection long before a single word is penned. It calls for moments of pause and countless questions—questions that linger, press, and demand answers before I could even commit to this journey. Why write? Why share these particular stories, and what do I hope readers will find within them? In this foreword, I'll share some of these questions, the conclusions I reached, and a few thoughts on how to approach this book as you explore its pages.

Why Write a Book?

In a world filled with books, you might wonder why write yet another one. I asked myself this many times before embracing the journey of writing this memoir. My motivation was simple: I felt that my story and the lessons I've learned could help someone who might need them and perhaps wouldn't come across a similar message elsewhere. They might connect with my book because of our shared background or through a recommendation from a friend.

Why Write a Memoir?

Then, another question arose: why a memoir? Memories are famously unreliable, and our recollections aren't always accurate. Yet, there's value in our remembered experiences and the meanings we attach to them. We gain the most from our memories when we're not overly attached to them. To me, this means recognizing three truths about our experiences:

1. An event happened.
2. We had an emotional reaction to it.
3. We created an interpretation of what happened.

That last part—our interpretation—isn't fixed; it changes over time, and as it does, it colors how we recall the event itself. Or, as the great philosopher Yogi Berra might say, "The past ain't never the same."

With this in mind, the events retold in this book are my imperfect recollections, shaped by time and perspective. I acknowledge that I may have forgotten or remembered things differently from others. I have tried to observe my story with as much objectivity as possible, aiming to recount what I saw, felt, and experienced with compassion for everyone involved.

Embracing Universality

My goal was to write a book that speaks to the common threads in all our lives, one that anyone—regardless of background—could relate to. I didn't want anyone to feel excluded. Yet, I realized that my background as a former evangelical Christian comes through, especially with the occasional Bible verse or mention of "God." While I don't view the Bible as an infallible guide, I respect its wisdom and draw from it as I do from other traditions. For inclusivity, I sometimes use "G-d" or other terms like Creator, Source, or Universe to represent a higher power. Although I aimed for consistency, you may find variations throughout.

I want to emphasize that belief in a Creator isn't necessary to benefit from this book. I believe in a creative force, but not an anthropomorphic deity waiting to judge or punish. Whatever your belief systems, you will find some value in the book.

How to Read This Book

I believe in the 80/20 principle—that 20% of effort often yields 80% of the result. When reading a nonfiction book, I wonder which parts I can skip and which are essential. For readers interested primarily in resilience, I recommend Chapters 8 and 9, which can stand alone.

If you're at a life crossroads and asking, "What's next?" or "Is this all there is?" Chapter 7 might be beneficial.

Chapters 1, 2, 7, 9, and 10 provide a meaningful framework for those who prefer to skip around. However, I hope readers who are tempted to skip sections will consider that each chapter contains insights that may be valuable when viewed within the context of the whole story. It's not just about the lessons I share; it's about the connections you may feel with the emotions, thoughts, and experiences woven throughout the journey.

If you find meaning in this book, I'd be grateful if you shared it with others or provided feedback.

Happy Reading,
Live the Power Within,
Sammy

CHAPTER 1

Birth of a Special Child
The Years in Haiti (1970–1980)

"In every real man, a child is hidden that wants to play."
— Friedrich Nietzsche

My earthly journey began in Haiti on April 4, 1970; my life, however, was shaped less by the place I was born in and more by the events transpiring in my family during the period before my birth.

These include the emigration of my aunt, Marie Andrée Bichotte, to the United States, as well as the rivalry between my mother (who we call *Manman*, which is Kreyol for "mother") whose given name was Liliane, and the mistresses of my father, Horacius. If we include my own birth, my father was responsible for conceiving close to twenty children, including seven with my mother.*.

My three older siblings on my mother's side were my sisters, Gladys and Euphonia nicknamed Foufoune (born in 1956 and 1957, respectively), and Sperkland, a son (born in 1959) who died before he turned a year old. Although I never knew him, he would somehow still manage to become part of my story.

In this chapter, I will try and share how the ways in which the events leading up to my birth would come to affect my life.

◆→ ←◆

My first ten years in Haiti unfurled within the blurred boundaries of a middle-class existence that was, in truth, defined more by the

---

*I am grateful that overall, I have a great relationship with my siblings that doesn't depend on whether we share the same mother or father.

1

wherewithal to eat each day than by any true financial abundance. We—a patchwork quilt family of nine who owned neither a car nor the standard status-marker of a black-and-white TV—were emphatically far from wealthy. However, we *were* well enough off to afford a maid, and although we *did* have electricity in the house, there was no running water, with our "bathroom" being a bathroom in name only, existing as little more than a humble outhouse at the end of the backyard.

While our living situation was a modest one, what truly placed us in the middle class was the privilege of having access to a private education. Public schools, I understood, were the domain of the very poor and *restavèks*—children from rural families traded to city households in exchange for scraps and survival accommodations.

Though treated as second-class citizens, those who were allowed any education—even in public schools or evening classes— were considered to have been fortunate. In Haiti's highly stratified social system, attending a public school simply wasn't an option for us. While we attended private schools, they were certainly far from the hallowed halls of the elite, such as the revered Saint Louis de Gonzague in Port-au-Prince—institutions that families like ours could only dream about.

Although we were not able to feast as similar mainstream American families did with their abundantly provisioned pantries, our privilege took on the humbler—but no less consoling—form of reliably looking forward to having three meals a day. Six days out of the week, our staple fare was yellow grits paired with hearty beans (black or red, in a thick *sos pwa*—or pea sauce–soup) or stirred directly into the grits. Sundays brought a welcome relief from the daily fare, with protein gracing our table in the form of chicken and rice replacing the inevitable grits. Weekday meals often featured a simple Creole *sauce (sòs kreyòl)*, its tomato base enlivened by bits of salty herring, which was more for flavor than sustenance.

Only twice can I recall my hunger gnawing through the predictable rhythm of the "three-meals-a-day" continuum: once, when I was six, *Manman* surprised us with a vibrant green papaya dish instead of our customary beans. It burst with flavor, unlike anything I'd ever tasted.

"Why haven't you made this before?" I exclaimed, my tongue still dancing with the sweet tang.

Her reply, which remains etched in my memory to this day, revealed an unsuspected insight into our actual life circumstances: "Papaya, son, is for those who have *little*. Today, it's all *we* have."

The second time, after Mother had left for Guadeloupe in 1977, my sister Gladys stepped in to juggle our needs. There was this one occasion (before *Manman* began regularly sending us a much-needed stipend) when beans filled our bowls—but without the company of the ever-reliable grits; a rude surprise not unlike that of an expected guest (*invité mal* élevé) who suddenly stands you up.

To a Western eye, our lives might have hinted at scarcity. For example: for us, leaving our plates empty was almost always the norm, and we savored each morsel, licking them clean in the privacy of our home. Sometimes, my younger siblings and I would strategically drop by the neighbors' as they were about to serve food. To do so was to risk being tagged as *visye*—colloquial Haitian for "deficient in moral integrity, teetering upon beggary."

Even at this early juncture in my childhood, pride had already become a fiercely burning ember within my breast. Almost any trigger (the sting of an unwelcome glance, the unvoiced censure etched in another's stare) had the power to eclipse any pangs of hunger I might have been suffering at the time—though, I confess, one twilight, hunger gnawed with a ferocity that refused to be quelled. Even my heroic determination to avoid the shame of begging ultimately bowed to its onslaught, and I soon found myself at a neighbor's door, humbled— waiting, yearning for the comfort of even a partial, steaming plate.

Despite what might have seemed to be a background of poverty, I never saw it that way; my childhood was in fact filled with joy, and I cherish my memories of life in Haiti. I enjoyed the liberty of playing outdoors without supervision for many hours, and once I had learned to read, I began immersing myself in books to my heart's content.

Those memories include playing soccer with makeshift balls fabricated from stockings filled with whatever happened to be available at the moment, such as discarded papers and rags. Having since played soccer with a real ball later in life after I had left Haiti, I can say from firsthand experience that the perhaps-dubious quality of the makeshift ball did not in the slightest compromise the joy, the fervor, or the many delightful antics resulting from the passionate pursuit of the sport.

One of these memorable events was the time an airborne soccer ball somehow managed to splash straight into a huge pot of *sos pwa* (black beans stew) that was simmering on the outside fireplace. With the cook's complicity, we unceremoniously removed the ball, wiped it clean, and tacitly agreed to say nothing to anyone who had not been a direct eyewitness to the event. Our ad hoc thinking at the time was, "What you don't know can't hurt you" (*Sa ou pa konin, pa ka touye ou*)—and so far as I have been able to ascertain, this served the highest good in this particular instance.

My next favorite game was marbles. We played on a variety of surfaces—some more level than others—as an implicit part of the game had to do with the nature of the surface one was required to negotiate at the time, mandating that you have different kinds of shots in your repertoire for striking your target.

While I enjoyed actively playing the game, there was also a certain vicarious pleasure in watching older, more skillful players in action as they made incredible hits. The infinitely shifting strategizing required for marbles brought me so much joy that for a long time, I kept a jar of them front and center on my desk.

4

The girls played a game that we called *osslè* (or *osselet* in French) which involved using five pieces of bone fashioned from goat knuckles (which I would later learn, while writing this book, is called "knucklebones" in English, and was played as far back as Ancient Greece, where it was called *astragaloi*—meaning "divination dice").

The game made its way across the different continents, adapting itself to local customs along the way. It consisted of sending a piece into the air and then (while it was aloft) quickly turning the other pieces to the right side before picking them up—a progenitor of sorts to the 20th century game of "jacks" in the West. One begins by picking up one piece at a time while throwing one of the five pieces in the air; then two pieces at a time; then three pieces at a time; and then all four pieces. Should the airborne piece fall to the ground, you lose your turn. Once the pieces are turned the way a player wants and they find themselves unable to pick up the incremental number of pieces that they are up to, they lose their turn.

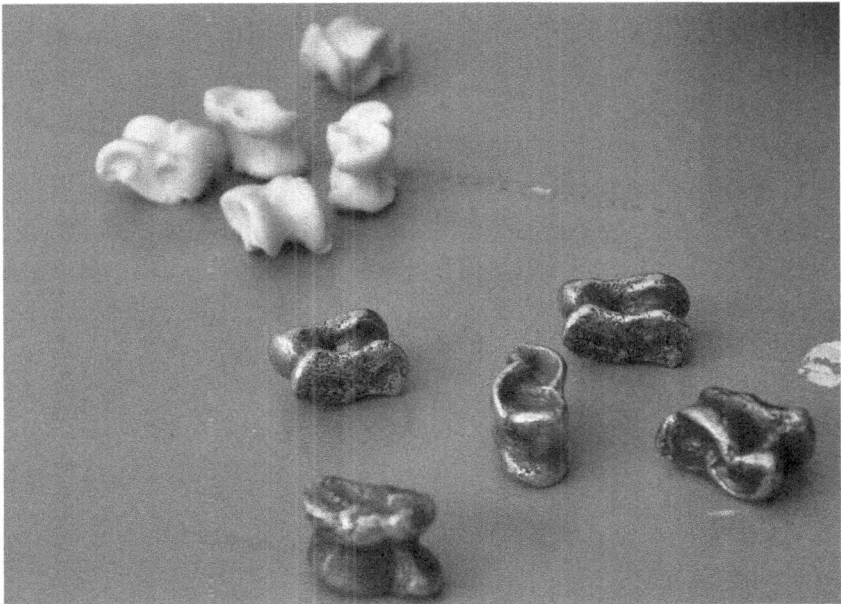

Picture of "osslè" pieces by Roland Zh, used under Creative Commons License.

While boys were not forbidden to play *osslè*, it turned out that the girls often possessed more finesse and were able to throw a piece in the air and quickly turn or pick up their pieces without the airborne piece crashing down too soon. Like many games in Haiti, you didn't have to be an active participant to enjoy it. Being a spectator and commenting on the game—or even giving advice as to what you would do if you possessed the skills of one of the players—was equally enjoyable.

Another game that favored girls was jumping ropes. I don't remember ever going past a count of three. On the other hand, I would often be amazed at the girls' ability to become one with the rope, jumping in whatever direction and for however long they wanted to, while two of their colleagues rotated the rope from each end.

When it came to playtime, evenings were special. Some of the most memorable sessions included the game of riddles, which we called *devinette*—mental puzzles which were followed or inter-spaced with various stories that I believe are unique to Haiti. The riddles themselves were not that different from ones one might hear in Western culture. However, the way in which we spoke these riddles, and the atmosphere in which we narrated them, fostered a different level of fun.

Our riddles started with the person about to give the riddle saying, "Krik," and everyone else responding, "Krak". Someone would say, "Krik", then we would reply, "Krak," at which point they would share a riddle they had heard somewhere or that they had made up.

One of the riddles I recall hearing was:

"Krik,"

"Krak,"

"What animal walks on four legs in the morning, two legs during the day, and three legs late at night?"

When I got older, I would recognize this riddle as the one from Ancient Greek mythology that the Sphinx would issue to men who failed to solve it before it killed them.*

Such fictional stories (*kont*) or real stories—some hard to believe—were part of the entertainment that filled our evenings. These stories often included fictional characters such as Bouki and Ti Malis, characters I believe might be unique to Haiti. The latter is the conniving and smarter of the pair, while the former is the forever gullible victim of many tricks. The *konts* I liked most were the ones that included singing.

One of those stories was about a girl who ate some oranges and was threatened with an unknown punishment by her stepmother. She went to her mother's grave, and while weeping there on the grave, a couple of orange pits that happened to be stuck to her clothing fell to the ground, where a tree started growing.

The young girl began to sing:

Ti zoranj grandi, grandi ti zoranj
Ti zoranj grandi, grandi ti zoranj
Belmè pa Manman, ti zoranj
Small oranges grow, grow small oranges
Small oranges grow, grow small oranges
Stepmother is not Maman, little orange

With that song, she influenced the orange tree to grow and harvested some oranges to bring to her stepmother. In the end, her stepmother persuaded her to confess how she had managed to get the oranges—but due to her avarice, she conveniently winds up exploding in the end.

All Haitian stories culminate in creative endings that attempt to explain how it was that there happened to be an eyewitness who

---

*The answer given by Oedipus who answered this riddle in Greek Mythology is that it's a human being. He walks on four legs as a baby, then he learns to walk on two feet, and then in old age walks with a cane, so he can be said to have three legs.

ultimately came to be the narrator. For example: for the orange story, you might come up with something like the following:

"*Mezanmi* (i.e., '*mes amis*'—my friends), I went to the market where this old woman was selling oranges and I told one of the vendors, 'It's true the stepmother was an evil person, but maybe she didn't have to die.' When I said that, the vendor told me to mind my own business and gave me a huge kick in the posterior that propelled me here in order that I would be able to share this story with you."

There were also true stories (perhaps unbelievable, but nevertheless true—at least according to their narrators). The ones I liked most involved encounters with werewolves (*lougawou*) or secret societies called *sanpwèl* that roamed the streets at night. There was one story, based in our hometown *Croix-des-Bouquets* (a commune in the Ouest department of Haiti that includes Port-au-Prince) and told by *Manman*, of a *lougawou* who had killed many children and who, on her deathbed, started confessing to so many misdeeds that her family members had a doctor administer a preparation to her to accelerate her death.

I also heard many stories about men who had been so brave as to be outside during the wee hours of the night and encountered *sanpwèl* bands or mysterious animals guarding bridges, crossroads, and other pathways and, by minding their own business or boldly asserting their right to be on the road, were able to pass without harm.

I was fascinated by these tales, and too young to question their authenticity. In hindsight, if I were to believe *every lougawou* story that I've been told, I would have had to admit that Haiti had historically harbored the highest per capita population of werewolves of any country on Earth. It is well known that we Haitians love to put pepper and other spices into a story (*pwav ak epis*). Similarly, there is no question that some of those stories are spiced up with superstitions and exaggerations.

However, I have my own story of *lougawou*. In *Croix-des-Bouquets*, my mother and father had separate houses. As I understand it, the dwellings came down to them from their respective families through inheritance. In the front yard of *Manman's* house was a huge almond tree *(pye zanmann)*. I remember vividly one particular night when a crowd primarily made up of men carrying makeshift lanterns that included slow burning pine torches *(bwa pin)* brought a woman with them that they accused of being a *lougawou*. Apparently, they had caught her in the act.

Someone retelling that story might say they have seen a *lougawou* with their own eyes, and that might be technically true. In my case, keeping an open and critical mind, I can only say for sure that a woman whom they *claimed* to be a *lougawou* was caught and brought under our almond tree, and that I witnessed the event.

Because my access to a wide variety of books was quite limited, I devoted much of my time to exploring the Bible, as it was always available—especially the captivating tales from the Old Testament. For an inquisitive young child like me, the Biblical narratives (such as David's battles and rise to kingship, Jacob's deceit, the great flood, or Joseph's saga) were enthralling adventures.

But the center of that remembered world is filled with the warmth of a very loving home, for even from my earliest recollections, I always felt cherished and important. There was, however, one person who had the capacity to instill fear in me: our next-door neighbor, Madame Eugène. She was deeply religious and highly respected by the other women in the neighborhood.

Her methods of disciplining her children were harsh; treatment that would be considered child abuse in the US or elsewhere. Her youngest son, who was 16 or so, would be tied down for her ritual beatings. His screams during these chastisements would echo through the neighborhood, sending chills down my spine. Occasionally, when my mother had errands to run and my older sisters were absent, she would ask Mrs. Eugène to watch over me,

9

saying, "Neighbor, don't break any bones, don't draw any blood, but if he misbehaves, discipline as you think necessary."

Madame Eugène never actually laid a hand on me. The mere thought of being disciplined by her was enough to keep me more than well-behaved.

Another figure who was capable of invoking fear in me apart from Madame Eugène was my father; I grew up hearing tales about his stern nature and how harsh he was toward my mother. Yet, he never physically harmed or threatened me. My father had a presence that commanded respect and caused you to think twice about crossing him.

This sense of respect extended even beyond our home, as well. As he was the brother of a twin who had passed away early, the people in our hometown of *Croix-des-Bouquets* attributed mystical abilities to him, due to mythologies at large in Voodoo lore. These included being able to cast spells without having to visit a *houngan* (which is to say, a male voodoo priest) and being protected by voodoo spirits that made him somehow invulnerable to spells that might be cast by enemies. My father would also claim that he could be in several places at the same time, and that if he wished to, he could travel wherever he wanted by using a matchbox as his means of transportation.

It was only later in life that I understood that he possessed— or at least demonstrated—no such powers, and that it was rather the case that he relished the respect that stemmed from people's unfounded fears. This skepticism about my father's powers is not shared by all my siblings. Some still believe he had special powers.

I distinctly recall two instances in which I had an unsought opportunity to witness my father's harshness firsthand. I was around six or seven years old at the time of the first occasion; my mother was out of money, coinciding with my dad's payday at Hasco, the railroad company where he was employed transporting sugar cane. I'm not certain about her reasoning, but perhaps she sent my sister and me along in hopes that our presence might soften my father's heart.

We needed to take two Haitian *tap taps* (converted pickup trucks serving as public transports) to reach his workplace—but unfortunately, she didn't even have enough money to cover both our fares. As a result, we took a *tap tap* for the initial part of the journey and then had to walk the remaining distance.

To this day, that trek remains the longest I have ever walked for reasons other than pleasure, and I have walked a considerable amount in my life. I vividly recall my sister and I being the only ones on that road, under Haiti's intense sun, our stomachs empty, and so thirsty that the dryness in our throats was palpable. Upon reaching our destination, we found out, ironically, that my father wasn't there. We had been unaware of his work situation since he did not live with us despite being married to my mom

Exhausted and unable to return the same way we had come; we explained our situation to my dad's supervisor. Although it was against the rules, he compassionately decided to give us an advance on my dad's salary.

When my dad next visited us, he was furious. This was my first time witnessing him in such a mood. My mother tried to justify her actions by explaining she saw no other way to feed us, but this explanation did not appease him. What truly astonished me was his indifference to the arduous journey that I, as a young child, had to endure in this situation. Even at that young age, it felt profoundly unfair that my sister and I had to endure such hardship just to implore my father for what should have been his willing financial support. I could never comprehend his reaction—especially his complete lack of concern for the suffering his youngest children were going through.

On the second occasion I witnessed his unkindness, I was not directly involved. I was about eight or nine years old at the time and staying with my Aunt Vierge (my father's sister). He was living with his young girlfriend, Woulone, who was barely 22 years old. They resided in a house that shared a large backyard with my aunt's place, where other family members also lived. Despite his proximity, I hardly remember seeing my father during that summer vacation, nor can I recall him spending any one-on-one time with me.

However, I do remember one afternoon dictinctly: father came home and saw Woulone playing a board game called *kay* with my cousin Jocelyn (my father's nephew) and other cousins. The game involved a board with 2x6 holes in the ground, using pebbles as pieces, and I was sitting nearby watching them play. Jocelyn, older than me, was about 18 at the time.

Upon witnessing this scene, my father became very angry. He said that he thought it was inappropriate for Woulone, as his partner, to be indulging in such childish activities, and that he felt disrespected by her behavior. Although I might not have realized it at the time, it's now clear to me that my father's anger stemmed from jealousy about Jocelyn.

But my father and Ms. Eugène were outliers in my otherwise positive childhood memories. During my younger years, I often felt special—both due to the unique circumstances of my birth and the affection with which my grandmother treated me.

There was a significant age gap between my siblings and me. My sister, Gladys, was born in 1956, and my sister Euphonia (nick-named Foufoune) was born in 1957, making her 13 years older than me, who arrived in 1970. Even when one accounts for Sperkland (the son who was born after Euphonia in 1959 and died as a tod-dler), I was the only one born with such a gap between myself and an older sibling. My brother Jonas arrived in 1972, Stanley in 1974, and Ruth (my youngest maternal sister) in 1976. After she moved to Guadeloupe in 1977, my mother had two more sons with a different father (Camille and Alex) in 1980 and 1982, respectively.

The story behind the significant age difference between my older sister and me is quite remarkable.

For several years prior to my birth, my mother suffered from a mysterious illness. Her abdomen was unusually swollen and she experienced pain, but no doctor could accurately diagnose her condition. Initially, they suspected fibromyalgia. My sister has recounted to me how our mother sought various forms of healing, including a pilgrimage to Seau D'eau, a mystical mecca in Haiti known for its miraculous cures.

I grew up hearing that one of my father's girlfriends did not want me to be born. Rumor had it that she was trying to harm me in the womb, hoping to be the first to give my father a son, and she was the reason behind the mysterious death of Sperkland.

My mother regarded my birth as a miracle. She had turned to both medical and traditional Haitian remedies, but believed her recovery and my birth had both been divine interventions. She has shared several times the dream in which a voice told her, "You are not sick, you are pregnant. You will have a son and you should name him Samuel." Upon awakening, she wrote the name "Samuel" with charcoal, as instructed in the dream. The story of my mother's difficult pregnancy, including how she came up with my name, was told to me by my older siblings and cousins, who have confirmed it and added to the details.

This name "Samuel," given by what *Manman* believed to be an angelic visitation, was the name I was known by during my early life. It was only when I was about to leave Haiti for Guadeloupe that I discovered, upon viewing my birth certificate, that my father had named me "Jean-Guilmond" which I was told was to honor his father Raymond. Given the uniqueness of my name Jean-Guilmond, I have reasons to believe that my paternal grandfather, having lost his first grandson (my older brother Sperkland), desired this name as protection for me. Literally, the name "Guilmond" means "will protect" in German.

My birth played a pivotal role in my mother's conversion to Christianity. Being named after a prophet, Samuel, instilled in me a belief that I had been chosen for a special purpose. Once I learned to read, the Bible (being the only book available) captivated me—especially the stories of the prophet Samuel. I felt a connection to his divine calling, and eagerly anticipated my own. I believed I had special protection, having overcome the "dark forces" as purported by local legends of werewolves in *Croix-des-Bouquets* that allegedly sought to harm me after my birth.

This sense of divine shielding, coupled with being the first son of my parents' marriage, shaped my self-perception as a leader—particularly a spiritual one. By the age of five, I was already playing at being a preacher. At eight, I delivered my first sermon during a series of evangelistic meetings in Leogane, in Southern Haiti. Interestingly, in my youth, these evangelistic gatherings (which were geared toward gaining converts) were called "crusades," without any awareness of the term's historically negative connotations.

In addition to the extraordinary circumstances of my birth, the special treatment I received from my maternal grandmother, *gran* Thérèse, contributed greatly to my sense of being unique. Among my many cousins (I know of at least 41, with 13 from my eldest aunt DieuDonne alone), I was the sole one chosen to be her godson. In a predominantly Catholic country like Haiti, this status held significant meaning. While the common outsiders' view of Haiti as a voodoo-practicing culture—an overhang from its African origins—my experience growing up was that most people, including my extended family, were Catholic. The exceptions within my own family were my mother and one of her sisters, Aunt Eunide, who were evangelical Christians—specifically Seventh-day Adventists.

My grandmother was a spirited woman who wasn't shy about playing favorites, and as her godson, I often found myself being the privileged recipient of this personal bias. I remember times when she would wake me from sleep, tired but not grumpy, to ensure I had a full plate of her cooking. Sadly, not all my siblings share similar fond memories of our *gran*. To this day, my sister Foufoune harbors resentment toward her, believing the preferential treatment I received and the disparity in how she and other siblings were treated stemmed in part from their darker skin tone, which was inherited from our father, of whom grandmother was distinctly less than fond.

Foufoune often recounts a particular incident in which *gran* Therese lost something. She then lined up all the cousins who were old enough to be considered suspects and used a makeshift pendulum—a key dangling from a thin string over a partially filled glass of water—as her "truth divining rod." As she moved from one cousin to another, she would repeat with a voice of certainty the dreaded commands to the pendulum: "*Par St Pierre, Par St Paul, dis moi la vérité*" ("By St Peter and St Paul, tell me the truth"). The pendulum would remain still until reaching the supposedly guilty party, where it would then swing wildly—and in this instance, it chose Foufoune. *Gran* accused her of the theft with unalterable conviction, claiming that her pendulum never lied. My mother, following grandmother's insistence, disciplined Foufoune.

Reflecting upon my childhood, I see the impact my birth narrative had in shaping the course of my life. It set the stage for me to feel empowered to achieve extraordinary goals, a narrative predestined even before I was born. In a way, I was like a divine child, shielded by higher powers from malevolent forces, akin to Harry Potter—but in my case, the protective magic started much earlier, a decade before conception, while I was still *in utero*.

The way people regarded me early in life as someone special, coupled with the belief in a unique calling attributed to the way I was named, likely influenced my self-perception and contributed significantly to the unusual level of confidence I possessed. This was not merely confidence in my own abilities, but also in the reassurance that when my own efforts fell short, there were higher powers upon which I could rely for support.

I have always been intrigued by other characters, both historical and fictional, who were convinced by their parents or guardians that they were special figures (such as Samuel of the Bible, Alexander the Great, Harry Potter, John the Baptist, and even Jesus). While I recognize that a part of the confidence they exhibited likely stemmed from innate qualities, I am also convinced that a significant portion of it was nurtured—deriving from the belief instilled by their parents or others in their world of their specialness. This nurturing undoubtedly played a crucial role in the full expression of their confidence and potential.

The privilege of being born as a "special one" is, in my view, one of the greatest gifts any child could receive. It's a gift that continuously enriches one's life, equipping one to tackle any challenges that might arise. Looking back, I wish I had imparted this belief to my children, and I hope that as a society, we can learn to view every birth with the same reverence and joy we associate with the nativity of baby Jesus, much like the sentiment expressed in the lines of the French carol:

> *Il est né, le divin enfant*
> *Chantons tous son avènement*

> (He is born—the divine child
> Let us all sing to his coming)

I yearn for a world in which every child is assured they are—and is consequently treated as—the Divine Being they are, recognizing that our existence on this Earth is as miraculous as the odds each of us has had to overcome. Consider the immense journey of any human being: first, the survival of ancestors through wars, famines, natural predators, and other uncontrollable forces; and second, there is the remarkable (indeed, almost inconceivable) biological journey, starting as one singular survivor among hundreds of millions of sperm cells, braving the hostile conditions of the fallopian tubes, the acidic environment of the vagina, and the immune defenses of the female reproductive system.

Indeed, I was born a special child, and so were you—each of us a miraculous testament to the wonder of Life. Everyone carries what the theologian Duns Scotus calls "the imago Dei" (the image of God), with the potential to express the fullness of her love and creative power.

So, where do we go wrong? At some point, I believe that every human loses their childhood innocence and experiences rejection—a sense of not belonging or something being "off" with the world. This key turning point in life is something that should unite all humans, and we can all learn by sharing with each other how we lost that innocence, as well as the filtered lenses we have been seeing life through since that experience.

In the next chapter, I will share my story of how this innocent child from Haiti who loved everyone and felt loved chose to become a Lone Wolf.

CHAPTER 2

From the Trusting Child to the "Lone Wolf" (1976–1980)

"The ego is the false self—born out of fear and defensiveness."
— John O'Donohue

While there was always food on the table, we could never quite rely upon the quantity we sat down to. Some days brought abundance, inspiring the phrase "Marguerite brought good syrup," a Haitian colloquialism that referred to plentiful meals of high quality.

But there were also more than a few times when, despite the food quality, portions were minimal to modest at best, leading to slightly less laudatory phrases referring to Marguerite delivering "good syrup—but in meager quantity." These occasions were typically heralded by a shift from the usual grits to rice or chicken, but in less than satisfying amounts.

Growing up, I puzzled over Marguerite's identity, imagining her as a benevolent spirit akin to a fairy godmother overseeing our earthly nourishment. I later discovered that Marguerite was also the name of my maternal grandmother Thérèse's older sister, who had raised her. In the convolutions of my magical thinking, this became a revelation which suggested that in my family, "Marguerite" might not only symbolize "a mythical provider," but could also be a direct reference to my great aunt who, as the primal caregiver, would always seek to ensure her siblings were fed.

Occasionally, our evening meal preparation would begin unusually late—sometimes not until after dusk, when we would have our main meal. Usually, our dining routine included breakfast, a substantial lunch between noon and 2:00 p.m., and a lighter supper of porridge (often made with white flour and occasionally replaced with fine corn flour, homemade plantain, or—more rarely—millet porridge). During times of scarcity, a simple soup with bread (either fresh or, just as often, stale leftover pieces) might tide us over until the late main meal, eliminating the usual porridge supper.

By the age of four or five, I started to notice the nuances of our cuisine, such as it was—particularly the preparation of beans, a staple in our diet. Soaking beans overnight was a practice whose importance I only truly understood when I began cooking for myself. This method was essential for reducing cooking time—a critical consideration when one had no access to modern cooking appliances. And if they weren't already on hand, the demand for fresh beans (like peas or *pwa chouch*, colored Lima beans) required someone to journey to the market, necessitating a layer of pre-planning to our meal management.

One day, during breakfast, when I inquired about the content of our lunch, my mother's response was firm: "Eat what's on your plate. Haven't I always provided for you?" Bizarrely, the sublimated intensity of her reaction caused her to launch into what struck me even then as an illogical train of thought, in which she spoke of "doing the impossible," such as turning water into butter *(bat dlo pou fè bè)*—a metaphor for creating a miracle—to ensure we were fed. Looking into her eyes, I sensed her uncertainty about our next meal; it was clear that the poor woman had no clue from where it might come.

This wasn't the first time I had queried her about such concerns. Her previous responses had succeeded in reassuring me that the next meal *would* appear on the table, even though there was not yet any apparent evidence of it. But this time was different—it was as if my eyes had been opened. There was the sudden anxious realization of, "*Holy cow*—she doesn't have a clue either!" And there was also anger. I wanted to scream, "I'm not *that* stupid!" To this day, I tend to suffer from such an overreaction when I sense that others are attempting to deceive me or are taking me for a fool.

In retrospect, it seems clear to me, despite my assurance of being unique, that my obsessive focus upon such concerns betrayed that I was the victim of a deep insecurity about our—or at least *my*—welfare and possibly even overall survival. With this sober realization, my awareness of our financial situation came much more clearly into focus. I began comprehending my mother's challenges in attempting to provide for us.

In Haiti, where formal day jobs were scarce, my mother's income derived from a mixed bag of sources, as my father's contributions were infrequent and meager, and barely began to address the needs of our large family.

Fortunately, my Aunt Andrée, who had emigrated to America in 1970 shortly after my birth, sent us regular support. This was critically vital aid, as her three older children, Wayne, Wagner, and Berda (also known as Marcelle) lived with us.

Manman's other lifeline was her small merchant business. She would travel to the provinces, purchasing agricultural goods wholesale and then selling them to other merchants or directly to friends and family. Unfortunately, the income from this endeavor was inconsistent. When money ran low, she'd borrow from friends and family—and if that failed, valuables like radios or watches went to the pawn shop. All too often, the cold silence of our charcoal stove spoke eloquently about her failed loan attempts.

Manman's business also faced challenges in the form of unreliable customers. Promises of "I'll get you your money soon" did not always translate into reality, leaving her futilely chasing after unpaid debts.

When I came to realize that even *she* was uncertain about the source of our next meal, it triggered a profound shift in my worldview, a moment I describe as my "loss of innocence," catapulting me into a path of fostering self-reliance and propelling me into what I term my "Lone Wolf" phase.

This worldview would eventually unravel the illusory security of my naïve childhood faith and revolutionize my entire approach to life.

It took the form of an extreme dedication to academics and an almost evangelical adherence to discipline. The reason was simple: I saw education as my one-way ticket out of the humiliations of poverty.

By the age of six, I was left to roam the streets and play unsupervised—and most striking of all, I was never once queried by anyone as to where I had been or with whom I had been playing.

At seven, I would walk the two miles to school with my friends (not an unusual achievement at the time and the norm for most of my schoolmates). And while some children might elect to cut class now and then, such temptations would never even enter my mind. The adults around me trusted me 100% to self-manage.

This determined self-responsibility, however, still didn't protect me from the consequences of various childhood misadventures. At six, I secretly indulged in homemade Haitian coconut punch (*crémasse*) paired with a unique, locally made peanut butter—a combination far removed from the reach of any supermarket our family could afford, had any even existed at the time.

Unlike the industrially mass-produced store brands, Haitian peanut butter is crafted manually from grilled peanuts, hot pepper, and oil. The grilled peanut maintains an inviting and persisting aroma while the hot pepper sends some pleasant zings to the palate as the buttery mix caresses it. The blend of its texture with the *crémasse* was a delight I couldn't—and didn't even seek to resist, leading to suspicion unjustly falling upon my older cousins Wagner and Wayne rather than myself.

In revisiting the incident above, I don't recall that my cousins were ever disciplined at the time; they rarely were because their mother was an essential source of our income. And for that reason, I always felt that *Manman* treated them better than she did us.

Manman was always worried about the possibility that others might report back to Aunt Andrée that her children were being mistreated or that my mother was somehow mistreating them.

The sad part is that she overcompensated for this lopsided fear of perceived bias—and on this, my older siblings agree with me. My cousin Wayne, known to be a constant violator of the rules, would never receive any direct redress from my mother when he had done something egregious. Instead, she would wait and call upon Boss Émile (a family friend) to dish out the requisite physical discipline.

The second mischief I recall happening was when I was about eight years old: my mother had left for Guadeloupe, and I was visiting my sister Euphonia for a few days. She had married a man named Hudson a short time prior, and they had parented a young girl (also nicknamed Foufoune) who was about six years older than me. I calculate her age with some degree of confidence because I knew, from the sexual explorations that she initiated with me at the time, that she had to be in the throes of puberty.

Hudson had prepared some food for his family that contained pork lard, and as a Seventh-day Adventist, I didn't consume anything containing pork or certain fish (those without scales). But one day, my hunger must have gotten the better of me because somehow, when no one was watching, I helped myself to some of the food. Hudson, realizing that someone had partaken of it without permission, automatically assumed without questioning anyone that the young girl had done it. Despite her protests of innocence, he proceeded to use his belt upon her—a shocking episode in which she was beaten severely. Even more than fear, I believe it was shame that prevented me from coming forward to confess to the crime.

The cries of the innocent young Foufoune still haunt me to this day, whenever I happen to be reminded of this incident. She was screaming, "*M mandé padon, M mandé padon*" (or "I ask for forgiveness, I ask for forgiveness..."), but Hudson's fury did not relent, as he went on shouting back at her, "*Shut your mouth!*" ("*Feme djol ou*"). The translation would be considerably more derogatory, as *djol* refers to the anatomy of an animal—a rough parallel being the American colloquialism, "Shut your trap!"

Throughout the entire span of my life with her, I can remember only one occasion upon which I experienced physical punishment at my mother's hands. This, I believe, speaks of another, deeper layer to our relationship and her faith in me because, during that era, Haitian parents tended to assess their parenting skills based on their ability to discipline effectively.

The incident in question transpired on a Friday afternoon. At that time, being Seventh-day Adventists, we would observe the Jewish Sabbath, ceasing all activities from sunset to sundown, and engage in a customary ritual welcoming the Sabbath with singing and prayers. My mother's chosen song, *The Star on the Horizon is Descending (L'astre à l'horizon descent)*—a reference to sundown—still resonates clearly in my mind.

On that fateful Friday, however, I remained oblivious to her singing. In my six-year-old mind, I was convinced that her failing to call me to open Sabbath meant I was free to go on playing. Suffice it to say that our respective expectations of what constituted proper behavior markedly differed.

After she had completed the opening ritual, she grabbed a tree branch and wrought a memorable chastisement upon me. In her eyes, the Sabbath was sacrosanct, and the singing traditionally served as my cue to join the observance. Hence, my obliviousness had been interpreted as defiance—and beyond whatever excuse I seized upon to justify my behavior, perhaps it was.

When my mother left Haiti to migrate to Guadeloupe in 1977, I don't recall that I cried. Even as a seven-year-old, I understood this was a necessary period of separation, motivated by her need to provide for us and that we would eventually all go to Guadeloupe to join her.

Before she departed from Haiti, our cousins Wayne, Wagner, and Berda had moved to the US in 1975 to be with their mother, Aunt Andrée. So we naturally anticipated that we would be likewise reunited with our mother.

Having a parent overseas could be considered a mixed blessing. While you didn't have the presence of that mother or father, you had the assurance that you would be well provided for and eventually have an opportunity to emigrate to a country where you could live like a *gran neg*—a "rich black one." Only later, when I had become a father, did it cross my mind how heart-wrenching it must have been for a mother to leave her children behind in search of greener pastures on their behalf.

I know from experience that behind every story of a parent who is forced to leave their children in search of a better life in a distant land, there is something within the soul of each that is forever lost and can never be restored—the sacred opportunity to intimately participate in the never-to-be-recaptured days and years of that being's life.

Forced to act against their deepest instincts, such parents have no choice but to completely surrender control of their children, trusting that the Universe will provide the needed nurture in the form of a warm embrace or caring glance through the intercession of other unknown hands and eyes. This is what some who have experienced this separation termed "*chèché la vi, détwi la vi*"—or, seeking the unknown path leading to a better future, while in the process destroying a known path that includes love, nurture, and the certainty of empty stomachs.

Each lost moment "an unseen tear"... each forsaken year a little death.

During my mother's absence, my two older sisters, Euphonia (Foufoune) and Gladys, were my caretakers. My brother-in-law

Hudson and my younger siblings Jonas, Ruth, and Stanley joined my mother in 1978. He went first so that he could work to help support his wife, while Gladys, my older sisters, and I rejoined my mother in 1980.

Until her husband left, Euphonia had barely any time for me, even though she lived in a nearby separate home. Understandably, most of her time was spent with her husband as a newly married couple.

After her husband left, I only remember spending time with her when we would go together to religious services in special settings. Instead of going to the main church on Sabbath, she preferred to go to small informal home services or a place called "Sion" on a hill in a natural cave.

The latter was a place to which Christians from all denominations would go on pilgrimage to seek deliverance, crying out to the "Lord Almighty." The crowds (which usually consisted almost entirely of women) would come there to fast, often with only a piece of cloth—and some even with a sackcloth—to protect against the hardness of the uneven, rocky ground. My impression of their reasoning was the more impoverished your condition when you came (hence the sackcloth, as opposed to a proper blanket), and the hollower and hungrier you were (thus the fasting), the louder you wailed and the more likely that God would hear you. Attending these services with my sister imbued me with a sense of pride and accomplishment that I had been accepted into the ranks of adulthood. These were occasions during which I fasted like the grownups and endured long sessions of prayers that alternated with high-pitched songs of supplication.

My sister Gladys, although the oldest, was only 21 years old when *Manman* left. For some reason, my mother was very strict with her, much more so than my sister Euphonia. Gladys never had a boyfriend while *Manman* was in Haiti. While I wouldn't say that all hell broke loose with my *Manman's* departure, she went to church on Sundays instead of Saturdays and eventually met her boyfriend there.

With my sisters in their early twenties having to create their own lives without the benefit of a mother, I was left to my own devices. I went to school by myself, played when I wanted to, and interacted with whom I wished. No one checked my homework, asked me about my friends, or how my day had gone. While I would prefer to believe that my siblings had chosen to purposely leave me alone because they knew I could take care of myself, the reality is that they probably had their own fish to fry, and they felt that maintaining the home and seeing to it that I had a warm meal was all they owed me.

I do not resent my siblings for not cuddling me enough or for less than adequate supervision. The latter is precisely what I craved. I have always thrived upon and enjoyed autonomy. I can't imagine what it would have been like if I had had parents who didn't let me run free as my sisters did—let alone what life would have been like with "helicopter parents."

Perhaps I was born able to thrive autonomously; thus, being apart from my parents could be considered Life's gift, creating a unique set of circumstances that challenged me to become resourceful.

One lesson I learned early on is that although we may appear, by objective observation, to be alone in the world, we are in reality, always being supported by an unconditionally loving Creator.

My last memory before leaving Haiti is of attending a half-day fast on the Sabbath morning at the service leader's home, along with 20 or 30 others. After one of the prayers, the service leader told us that when we pray, it should be a two-way conversation with God, in which we should also give God time to reply. So, she had us hum a song while we listened for God to respond to us.

During this prayer, even though I was fully awake, I felt myself in a dream-like state in which, without seeing any face, I heard a voice saying to me: "You are going to be delivered, and you will see it today." Yet, I had no idea what this vision might mean.

When I went home, to my surprise, there was a man named Alexandre waiting there who had come to take me to Guadeloupe. I don't know how *Manman* had worked out the logistics for me to get a passport so quickly—but sure enough, within days, I *was* in Guadeloupe.

Later, I would learn that Alexandre was *Manman's* boyfriend, whom she must have met a few months after leaving Haiti. By the time I had moved to Guadeloupe, my mother already had a son by him—my brother Camille, who was born in 1978 (he passed away in 2018). Alexandre had a cousin who worked at the airport as an immigration officer and had arranged for us to arrive in Guadeloupe while he was on duty. In retrospect, I am not sure whether we even had a visa. During those days, travelers would be screened upon arrival and could be turned away if they didn't meet the entry criteria. But with Alexandre's cousin, we just breezed through immigration.

It is possible that *Manman* told my older sisters that she had taken a boyfriend. This is not something I would have expected her to share with me, a young son at the time. Later, when I was older, *Manman* confided that when she came to Guadeloupe, she felt that she had no choice but to accept into her life a man who could help her take care of her children and possibly help bring them into the country.

When she spoke about the situation, I could see the sense of shame on her face for having chosen to "live in sin". Given her situation, she was no longer attending church. However, she still took pains to make sure *I* did. This wasn't the case for my younger siblings. The implicit message was that in her eyes, I was Samuel, the chosen one of God and that it was my divine responsibility to go.

For my part, she had no reason to be ashamed. In the view of the Adventist church, her willingness to risk sacrificing the promise of eternal life caused me to appreciate her selflessness on our behalf and to love her even more.

Until my late thirties, I attributed the persona of "The Lone Wolf"—otherwise known as "the control freak" compelled to take charge of his life because he couldn't even trust his parents—to the financial stresses they struggled with. Perhaps, this persona was shaped most profoundly by that watershed moment when I realized, despite her reassurances, *Manman* was at a loss as to how she was going to feed me.

Being driven by the insecurities of my childhood became the psychospiritual "fuel" I needed to pursue and achieve my goals for success. From puberty on through high school, college, and then into my professional career, I pushed myself, vowing that I would create the future as I wanted it to be—and that nothing and nobody would stand in my way. After all, when a lone wolf is hungry, who or what would wish to stand in his way?

Before I reached the age of 40, I began to have insights that enabled me to view the events of my childhood from a different perspective—which is to say, I no longer believed that I needed the "story" of "what had happened to me" to propel me forward. Instead, I opted for an alternative interpretation: no matter how desolate the situation appeared, I possessed the intuitive ability to "turn lemons into apple juice," even when everyone else is only expecting lemonade.

When I say we can turn lemons into apple juice, people often ask me: "So how do you do that? How do you turn your lemons into apple juice?"

My typical response is, "Well, you could sell your lemons," or you could simply ignore them and start from a different premise that would be like.ier to give you apple juice.

I never cease being amazed at how literally humans take the notion that life somehow actually does give us "lemons" and that limits us to drinking only lemonade. I believe it is equally valid that in every situation where such challenges present themselves, there is always the possibility of a "silver lining"—an unseen benefit we can leverage to bring us to where we wish to be.

One of the most common excuses people use to rationalize not going after what they truly want is lack of money. For example, they can't open a business because "You need money to make money." But I would argue that whatever apparent limitations we believe Life may have given us (such as not being born into an affluent family) may exist because Life wants us to realize that we don't necessarily need to rely on those parents, a rich uncle, or anyone else for that matter, to become a business owner.

I am by no means denying that some people (like myself) are born into more challenging conditions than others. Still, I *am* saying that, by virtue of my own experiences, there are *no* external circumstances that can stand in the way of us fulfilling our dreams. That which lies within us—the gifts with which we come into this world—is greater than any storms that might come against us from the outside. In my case, this gift is the ability to see what *can* be, no matter how desperate the current situation appears to be.

The lesson I have lived thus far, which I was unable to articulate until my late thirties clearly, is that our future does not depend upon our past, no matter how traumatic it may have been, nor does it depend upon our external circumstances in the present.

My life has taught me that we all have access to an inner power and abundant resources to create the life we dream of having. Part of that abundance of resources would come in the form of an escape from Haiti to emigrate to Guadeloupe. Chapter 3 describes my first few years on the island.

.

CHAPTER 3

The Care and Feeding of the
Lone Wolf (1980–1985)

"The soul that sees beauty may sometimes walk alone.
But we are never truly alone; the divine is always with us."

— Anonymous

Upon my arrival in Guadeloupe in 1980, I discovered that my mother had already welcomed two new siblings into the world: Camille, who was born in 1978, and Alex, who arrived in 1980, just a few months before my arrival on the island. My mother lived in a relatively spacious house with at least three bedrooms equipped with electricity and water. However, the bathroom was situated outside—a typical setup for many regional homes at the time.

Alexandre frequently clashed with my sister Gladys, leading her to move out shortly after my arrival to live with Aunt Eunide, one of our mother's older sisters on the island. Meanwhile, Euphonia and her husband had settled in a neighboring town about an hour away—a journey that today takes only 25 minutes.

With the departure of my older sisters, I suddenly became the eldest at home, tasked with caring for five younger siblings—Jonas, Stanley, Ruth, Camille, and Alex. This new role brought with it a significant amount of responsibility. My mother earned her living by purchasing wholesale clothing, bags, and accessories, which she sold door-to-door. Initially, she gained these goods through contacts who regularly traveled to places like Panama or Curacao, but by 1980, she had enough money to delegate these purchasing duties to Alexandre. Her business model was appealing because it saved her customers the trip to *Pointe-à-Pitre* or *Basse-Terre*, the island's commercial hubs. Additionally, offering goods on credit added value, allowing people to enjoy immediate ownership of desirable items and pay later.

My mother dedicated most of the time, six days a week, to her sales, with Alexandre chauffeuring her on these day-long endeavors. During the school year, she cooked for us before leaving—but in her absence and on school-free days, the cooking duties fell to me.

I developed my culinary skills through careful observation. Unlike when we lived in Haiti, our diet in Guadeloupe could include rice and beans daily, along with other food items that we usually didn't have access to. Progressively, my cooking repertoire expanded to include pasta with beans, dumplings made from flour cooked in dry beans, and dishes featuring roots and green bananas, often accompanied by creole sauce and meat. Initially, my mother would prepare the meat marinade—a crucial step—before I took over the cooking chores.

My mother's relationship with Alexandre was fraught with various stresses and lasted only about 18 months after my arrival. His need for control and dominance over my immigrant mother was easily noticeable. My mother initially lacked legal documentation despite having two children born in Guadeloupe. However, the power dynamics shifted about a year after our arrival as she gained regular residency status, which enabled her to travel to Curacao to make her purchases independently. Alexandre relished these trips for the opportunity to bring back luxury items like choice bottles of Johnny Walker whiskey, although he never appeared inebriated to me. Yet, his excessive drinking, combined with a formidable physique and temper, instilled fear in us all—especially my mother.

Somehow, my mother managed to move us out of our previous home and into a new one in the nearby town of Abymes without Alexandre's knowledge. We settled into a modest two-bedroom house with a spacious living room, and because of the lack of furniture, we transformed it into an indoor playground. Jonas and I often played soccer there. The house had electricity but lacked indoor plumbing; instead of a bathroom, we used buckets we emptied into a communal latrine maintained by the municipality, a short five-minute walk away. Despite the simplicity and challenges of our living conditions, this place was beaming with peace and love.

One day, my mother handed me a few bills—about one hundred francs (a significant amount for a 12-year-old). When I questioned her, she replied, "Because you're my son, and this is what I can give you." Her words were few, but her eyes conveyed deep love and satisfaction for being able to provide something meaningful to me.

At 12, while living in Abymes, I began taking on adult responsibilities. My mother was often away, working hard to support us. She would leave early in the morning and return late at night. As her confidant and co-captain, I managed the household in her absence, ensuring my siblings were well cared for. I adopted the practice of preparing more food than necessary and anticipating unexpected guests—a habit I maintain to this day.

Our relationship was such that my mother kept few secrets from me. Our neighbor Maryse, a single mother with several young children, occasionally relied upon us for necessities. One day, I noticed her face was bruised and swollen. Without my asking, my mother shared that Maryse sometimes went to *Pointe-à-Pitre*, the capital, to meet men who would pay her in exchange for her company. One such encounter had led to a violent assault. My mother's tone was neither judgmental nor condescending; she presented the facts straightforwardly. Although I was too young to grasp the implications of Maryse's actions fully, it was clear that she resorted to these measures as her means of providing for her children.

Less than a year after we moved into the house in Abymes, *Manman* would confide another secret: she had obtained an American tourist visa and was planning to reside there permanently. This was in 1982, two years and a few months after I had joined her in Guadeloupe. She wanted this information to remain secret because she feared that her former partner Alexandre might try to prevent her from leaving the island.

When *Manman* left Guadeloupe, it did not mean the cessation of my continued growth toward adulthood; instead, it accelerated it. There was no crying or time to process other emotions—I understood and accepted that this needed to be done, as she feared for her safety in Guadeloupe, and America offered her a better chance to earn enough money to take care of my younger siblings and me. On our end, we had to go about life.

When *Manman* left, my younger siblings and I (except for Camille and Alex) moved in with my sister Euphonia and her husband Hudson. They parked a food truck in *Parque de La Victoire* (Victory Park), located in *Pointe-à-Pitre* (the Capital). As the older brother, I was often called upon to help. There were many times when I would be the only one in the food truck. Hudson and my sister trusted me to put the fried dough (prepared beforehand) into the hot oil, sell the cold bottles of Heineken, and handle the money. Between 1982 and 1985, when I was helping on the truck, *Place de la Victoire* would be unlit, and prostitute gay men would rendezvous with their clients in this area.

How do I know this? Through the conversations that were had openly virtually in front of me. One of the gay men—*Petit Frère* (Little brother)—was of Haitian descent and a friend of Euphonia. He was very open to talking about his sexual life. Because of my Christian upbringing, one might expect that I would despise *Petit Frère*, given that he was practicing what, according to the Bible, was an abomination. Still, I did not harbor any disdain or hate toward him. I felt sorry for him.

My sister had explained to me that when *Petit Frère* was in Haiti, an American tourist had introduced him to homosexuality by plying him with money and gifts, such as a BMX bike that was the envy of many boys in the neighborhood. He would show off and do all kinds of tricks. He wore nice clothes and always had money, so everyone—including his parents—closed their eyes to the situation. It was with the help of this American tourist that he had been able to make his home in Guadeloupe. For me then, *Petit Frère* was a victim, though now, in hindsight he never took a woman even while in Guadeloupe; I even find myself questioning whether he wasn't born gay or at least bisexual. Part of my reasoning is that while there was a financial incentive to have gay sex in Haiti, he did have other means of earning money in Guadeloupe.

Within walking distance of Victory Park was an area known as *Carrénage*, which to this day in 2024 is home to a bunch of dilapidated houses where mainly foreign women engage in prostitution. *Petit Frère* offered several times to pay for me to be initiated into my sexual experience. While I knew I liked women due to my early interactions in Haiti, I had fallen madly in love with several girls in my class and had a massive crush on my sixth-grade English teacher, who was stunningly beautiful. But I wasn't mentally ready to step into a sex act. Years later, I've asked myself if *Petit Frère* was trying to test if I was gay or simply because he was introduced to sex early, he believed I should be as well; I think it was the latter and that there was no ill feeling in it.

Of course, I now realize that *Petit Frère's* conduct would be classified as child abuse. While I don't condone his actions, he never touched me physically or implicitly gave me any indications that he had any interest in me. I don't believe that he would ever have harmed me. He was not the cause of any emotional scarring on my part, although, with someone else of the same age, this could have been different. I've accepted that his actions were a product of what he was subjected to as a child.

One of the more vivid memories of being thrust too early into adulthood came with my niece Laurence, born to Euphonia and Hudson in 1983 during Mardi Gras. Mardi Gras (or Carnival) was by far the busiest time for the food truck. This celebration brings

35

the most people around Victory Park and the surrounding areas. Imagine thousands of people cavorting and dancing from early afternoon until far past midnight, endlessly hungry and thirsty. There was no way to provide enough food trucks to keep up with serving all of them.

My sister Euphonia went into labor on that Sunday of Mardi Gras, but that didn't stop my brother-in-law Hudson from dressing up as Harlequin in red and blue to go to dance carnival instead of supporting his wife or manning the food concession to take in as much money as possible. My sister Gladys and I went to work in the truck while Foufoune was in labor, and Hudson happily indulged in the delights of Carnival.

Although I was only 13, I knew this was utterly irresponsible and wrong. I didn't complain, nor was I resentful. But still, the voice arising within my heart was, "How *could* you?" This sense of duty was extreme in me, and I could not fathom that someone would leave their pregnant wife or abdicate their responsibility to earn money and provide for them in favor of Carnival.

I stayed with my sister Foufoune for another two years until 1985. During this time, I felt I was providing more support than I was being given. For example, during the municipal fairs, I would walk the fairground instead of going on rides and peddling fresh grilled peanuts to kids of all ages and their parents. When I finished selling a batch, I would come back to the truck to get another—one after the other. One of my fears was encountering one of my class-mates during those times. I could sense the shame of them seeing me as a street seller. It must have been Providence that this never happened. There was also the possibility that I was not always mak-ing eye contact with passers-by while calling out that I was selling "well-grilled peanuts," so I can't rule out that someone might have noticed me and been shocked, but decided to spare me the shame by averting their gaze.

Even during school days, I would go to the truck at night to help—but eventually, this began to show in the quality of my schoolwork. My grades started to suffer, at least in those classes where I was getting grades of B and C, whereas if I had only had a bit more time to study, I would have earned a solid A.

Besides the schoolwork, there were several times when I had been deprived of enough sleep, waking up with just enough time to put some clothes on and rush out the door to go to class. On two occasions, the physics teacher whom I had in the first period shamed me in front of the whole class, making me—and everyone else—painfully aware of my wrinkled clothes and "buggered" eyes.

The effect on my grades led me to accept an offer from my oldest sister, Gladys, to come and live with her. I resisted this for a long time because I knew I was my sister Foufoune's right arm. How would she manage without me?

At my sister Gladys's I got something I'd not had for a long time—structure. When I joined her, she was starting a young family. She had already given birth to her first child, my niece Miriam, whom she was raising in a two-bedroom apartment unit with her partner Dukingston, a much older man who could have been her father. This structured existence enabled me, perhaps for the first time, to count on the consistency of my meals and mealtimes, as well as when I would be able to sleep—and most importantly, my having dedicated time for homework.

The other structure they provided was the ability to practice my then-Seventh-day Adventist faith, which mandated no work activity between sunset Friday and sunset Saturday. With my sister Euphonia, even going to church was a luxury. I had no school on the weekends, and these were the busiest days for her food truck business.

But the greatest gift I received from living with my sister Gladys was the ability to rest both mind and body. My experience as an observer of the Jewish Sabbath has made me a firm believer that for our physical, mental, and spiritual health, we need to take regular breaks, including one day a week, to rejuvenate. Taking regular pauses is one of the key habits I recommend for optimal physical, mental, and spiritual health.

When I was growing up, the Sabbath meant idleness or spending most of the day on Saturday in church. Honestly, it often felt more like a burden than a source of enjoyment. Now, my rejuvenation practice includes a balance of rest and play. I take regular daily breaks for relaxation and activities I enjoy, and I dedicate one day each week to recharge, replacing the traditional religious Sabbath of my upbringing.

The other blessing from being at Gladys' house instead of Euphonia's was the ability to attend church regularly. Attending church was more than just creating normalcy or giving me any values (such as discipline) I might have lacked. What it provided me—which I never had until then—was the ability to build deep relationships with peers outside of the school setting.

From 1980 to 1985, between the ages of 10 and 15, the erratic nature of my life didn't even allow me to build friendships with kids in my neighborhood. I was so busy being another surrogate adult or caretaker for my younger siblings that I didn't have time for social activities. I formed a few friendships with a few kids I attended school with.

During our two-hour lunch break in junior high, I had a couple of friends with whom I would go out to play pinball. My school was too far away to go back home for lunch, so after gobbling up whatever I had brought, I would have time to burn. Additionally, Foufoune would give me some pocket money in return for helping her out with the food truck.

Now and then, this allowed me to buy a lunch sandwich and play pinball at least a couple of times a week at a local bar near our junior high. I never had enough money to play as much as my friends did, and many times—probably more than I realized—they either had to pay for me or let me play one of their three balls.

What I liked most about our church was that they had become a second family. Church service was only one of the many events where we interacted. There were also a lot of social activities, including Sunday soccer games and Saturday afternoon youth programs, that tended to be more relaxed, even though they would have a religious theme. I especially appreciated the time following these programs, when I could spend time with other people my age and just *be*, whether it was to chat about sports or, with increasing importance, girls.

My stay at my sister Gladys' house and my relationship with my siblings was far from perfect. Being forced upon her by necessity, taking care of us understandably compromised her ability to tend to her young family. As a result, she ultimately came to feel that she had sacrificed too much.

On the other hand, when Gladys took us in, *Manman* began sending money for us—none of which we ever saw. Before entering high school in 1986, I had reached out to social services and learned that they could assist with some grants that would help buy books and various other expenses. I completed all the paperwork—and I don't recall that a signature from my sister was even required; how-ever, when the money arrived by post, she pocketed all of it.

In high school, I worked to earn extra money by tutoring, and one summer, I went door to door selling weight loss products. Even these earnings were not safe from my sister's encroachments—but for me, this would be the last straw, compelling me to lie to her about how much money I was making to keep as much of it for myself as possible.

This allowed me to supplement the small stipend my sister would give me to buy books and supplies for myself and the younger siblings. The purchase of everyone except Miriam's books and sup-plies was one of the tasks assigned to me, which I gladly took on, but from the time she was old enough to attend school, my sister handled her purchases.

Purchasing supplies was not in itself a problem—at least not if I had been given the required funds to fulfill that necessity; but the most painful parts of the financial vise I had been caught in were the heart-wrenching decisions I was forced to make as to what would be kept in and left out. The latter were not just notebooks but often source texts. And while in Guadeloupe, books were freely provided up until high school, starting in junior high, items like companion workbooks for those source texts were the student's responsibility to provide.

The person most negatively impacted by this situation was my younger brother, Jonas, for although he tended to be in my shadow during his early upbringing, I knew then (and am convinced even more now) that had he been given the materials he needed, there is no limit as to what he could have accomplished. The crucial differ- ence was that he lacked my compulsive drive and ambition. If my intellectual capacity were to be likened to an engine with the ability to peak at 160 miles per hour, Jonas', by contrast, would have to be considered more like that of a generic family vehicle which, while appearing average, possesses an unsuspectedly powerful engine capable of providing a much more reliable and consistent means of transportation than my startling speedster.

The most heartbreaking aspect of the family situation after *Manman's* departure was the painful realization that the marginal love and care extended to us by both Gladys and Euphonia was, at best, erratic and far from even-handed. As a result of their inabil- ity to sufficiently care for all the children, the three youngest (Ruth, Camille, and Alex) were forced to go to *La Maison d'Enfance* ("The House of Childhood"), a public orphanage.

While the name conjures visions of a place in which the needs and sensitivities of childhood are nurtured and protected, I regret having to say that I saw it more as a place where childhood was incrementally stripped away and extinguished.

To an objective onlooker, it might seem that my older sisters were discriminating because the two youngest brothers were half-siblings whose birth father they palpably disliked. Still, this narrative would not explain the seeming abandonment of my sister Ruth.

Were anyone to have been able to step inside my soul and view the sad situation from my vantage point, they would have seen, glowing like an inextinguishable fire, my passionate longing to have been old enough to be able to gather all my siblings under one roof, in a warm and loving haven—and emphatically *not* the tear-drenched kingdom of the soulless *Maison d'Enfance.*

My total inability to help in any way filled me with unceasing shame and hopelessness. While my sisters had limited means, I believed at the time that if there had been enough love, the three youngest ones wouldn't have had to be placed under the soul-destroying "care" of the state. When I reflect on the situation, I have more empathy for everyone involved—including my older sisters.

I have empathy because, as painful as it is to admit, I didn't do as much as I could have at the time. Also, I need to consider that anyone would be overwhelmed by the responsibility of adequately caring for so many siblings.

I would understand if Ruth, Camille, and Alex, reflecting upon those times, were to conclude that I, too, did not do enough—and in all honesty, they would be right. Even as a minor, I could have visited them more often than the few times I did. Although the *Maison* had all the modern conveniences such as electricity and luxuries that we lacked, for all its many amenities, the so-called "Home for Childhood" was abidingly barren of Love, without which no human soul can indeed survive—much less thrive.

I wonder what the impact of being at *La Maison d'Enfance* was for these three younger siblings.

Here is the verdict. Camille died in 2018, just before he turned 40; he had predicted that he would not make it past this age. He was morbidly obese, and we found out after his death that he was diabetic. He ate whatever he wanted despite his conditions. Alex faces several challenges, the most apparent being his reliance on food and cigarettes, which seem to serve as coping mechanisms. He leads a largely insular life, with limited interactions even among family members, including us, his siblings. Ruth lives what appears to be a normal life with her husband of more than 25 years. I can only say that the nature of her relationships with the rest of us siblings is perhaps one of the many symptoms of brokenness that may run deeper than usual.

Ultimately, I see living with my sister Gladys as a blessing; it pro-vided the ideal training environment for a young lone wolf before being unleashed into the predator-filled forest and lurking perils of the adult world. There was enough structure (for zero structure would have been equally as perilous) and, simultaneously, enough autonomy to chal-lenge myself creatively.

To raise and cause a young human "lone wolf" to thrive requires, just as with actual wolves, a safe and reliable den in which to sleep, as well as the daily grounding of a routine and dependable nourishment.

So, one may wonder: is a lone wolf truly alone if his food and shelter are provided? No, not truly—not, at least, if one looks with 360-degree vision. The overwhelming dangers and disparities of human life cannot be successfully navigated through one's own devices, and even with the necessary infrastructures of home and family, the complete support we need doesn't necessarily come only from within those four walls.

In looking back at the period after my mother departed Guadeloupe for the US, I have come to see that I was supported and have concluded that even as a "lone wolf," I was, paradoxically, never truly *alone.*

In the next chapter, I will share some examples of the providential support I received.

CHAPTER 4

Never Alone...Even a Lone Wolf (1985-1989)

"You are never alone. You are eternally connected with everyone."
— Deepak Chopra

The expectations had been building up for months. It was the spring semester of my junior year in what, in French, is called college—but which equates to junior high school in America. We had been told that before the Fall semester was over, we would be doing "natation" (or swimming) as part of our physical education class. While I was excited because I had never gone swimming, I was also feeding off my classmates' excitement.

There were many reasons to be excited about "natation:" First, it was an opportunity to get out of our routine, boring gym, and being off-site—no matter what the reason—was welcome any day; secondly, this was like a weekly field trip in a school-chartered bus. While this may seem trivial, the delight of field trips of any kind was that the journey itself was as much fun as the destination. It was an opportunity to goof around and burst out singing folk songs like "*Lari zabim, té ni on vyé madam*" ("On the street of Abymes, there was an old lady")—i.e.:

Lari zabim. . .

—On the street of Abymes

Té ni on vye madam

—There was an old lady

Vyé madam la, té ni on kaz en pay

—The old lady had a house made of straw

Dèyè kaz la té ni on pyé piman

—Behind the old house, there was a hot pepper tree

Chalè a vyé fam la, tyé pié piman la chè

—The lady's heat killed the hot pepper tree, my dear!!!

With that last verse, our voices would rise into a crescendo. This is where the *gwo ka* (a goblet-shaped bass drum) would come in, and we would rise to the challenge by stomping, clapping, and banging on the seats or humming loudly, *"la la la la;" "la la la la la!"*

One of the things that has always fascinated me is the music and rhythmic cadence that naturally happened during these moments with my classmates. The harmony and synchronization of the tunes occurred naturally as if everyone had mastered a sheet of printed music, so much so that no conductor was necessary. Someone would naturally take the lead, and others would follow at the appropriate times.

The third reason for our excitement was that access to a swimming pool was a luxury. If one visits Guadeloupe now, there seem to be many swimming pools everywhere—facilities that are no longer the luxury of the upper middle class. During my time on the island, not only did I not know anyone who had a swimming pool, I'd never even seen one—even from afar, such as one might see now when passing by well-to-do homesteads.

Without a doubt, the municipal swimming pool we were going to was the only one that any of my classmates knew about, as well. While the admission cost wasn't prohibitive because it was not a local neighborhood facility, it was not so easy for any of us to get to, as it was situated in a sort of middle-class *quartier* that necessitated public transportation. But it was the only swimming pool I was aware of right up until the time I left Guadeloupe in 1989.

When we arrived at the pool, to say that a frenzy ensued would be an understatement. To efficiently use resources, we were grouped into two (and sometimes three) classes. Imagine 50 to 60 students converging on a space containing two swimming pools. Though the area was spacious, it still felt as if we were a swarm of bees landing on a single flower.

It was my first time at a pool, and though it may seem strange, the fact that I didn't know how to swim never even occurred to me. I saw my other classmates jumping into the pool, so I just jumped with no apprehension or afterthought.

When I jumped, I happened to be at the deep end of the pool—and upon plunging downward through the water, when my feet failed to touch the bottom, I started to panic. I struggled helplessly to claw my way back to the surface, which I could do a couple of times, but when I tried to yell, no one noticed me. I tried to grab a classmate's foot, but he fought me off. He would later tell me that he'd thought I was just playing.

Ultimately, I ran out of energy and ended up giving up and passing out. Before I lost consciousness, it was as if my short life had passed before my mind's eye, and all my dreams were going to be buried in this watery grave with me. This was it. I accepted the fact that I was about to die.

No one knows how long it was, but at length, someone found me at the bottom of the swimming pool. After I had given up and thought this was the end, I awoke to find myself surrounded by paramedics, teachers, and a bunch of other people. From what I could gather, they were trying to make sure that I regained consciousness before driving me to the hospital.

During my stay in the hospital, I recall that I was hooked up to a machine that removed water from my lungs. Given the mad buzzing of that machine (still in my head after all these years) and the amount of water it appeared to be pulling out of me, I have the lingering impression that I must have swallowed half of the water in the pool—or at least far more than a human body is supposed to be capable of containing.

In the end, I spent six days in the hospital. Friends and family members were astonished that I made such a speedy recovery. I had no permanent damage from the incident. The only thing that remains is a fear of water, which I have vowed to conquer at some point.

Based on conversations with classmates, I had spent a long enough interval underwater that it could arguably have killed me—or at least caused permanent brain damage. For me, this accident is a reminder that our life doesn't belong to us and is not ultimately *about* us; instead, we are about life. Whether one calls it a "guardian angel" or a "spirit guide," I am convinced that I could not have made it out of that pool alive without some help from beyond.

The incident at the pool was another turning point for me. It served as a second rebirth. As a 15-year-old on the verge of adulthood, it was an unmistakable sign that some higher power was supporting me. What could be the reason? I attributed it to the fact that I must have some unfinished business on this Earth.

In the Bible, two Psalms have a particular meaning for me: Psalm 23 and Psalm 139. In both of these, the author talks about God's presence even when facing death. Psalm 23 states: "Even though I walk through the valley of the shadow of death, I will fear no evil, for Thou are with me."

In Psalm 139, in answer to the question, "Where can we hide from the presence of the Creator?" (Verse 7), we are told, authoritatively, *no*where—even if we were to descend into the depths of hell.

I've taken these verses one step further as applying not only to physical death but spiritual death as well. But in the Bible, "spiritual death" does not mean annihilation or non-existence—but rather separation from God.

However, even this notion is an oxymoron (i.e., a self-contradiction), for can any living being or thing be said to be truly separate from its Creator?

Growing up in an evangelical church, the character of God that was most emphasized was that of a judge in dark robes, sitting high upon a throne and scrutinizing every one of our thoughts and actions. The God they preached to us was more like Zeus, ready to strike disobedient humans down with one of His thunderbolts. The answer to our prayers, not unlike the case of Santa Claus, is directly proportional to how good or naughty we were discovered to have been.

The idea that we had to bargain for protection or basic needs with an easily angered God forever on the brink of being royally out of joint about some sin or other never resonated with me. It was perhaps one of my most significant silent rebellions against the teachings of my church at the time. Instead, I had always assumed that if God said he would be present even in hell, it meant there is no sin that could separate us from him.

This conviction of an omnipresent Creator keeping a vigilant eye over us has always been a key tenet for me. Some have accused me of being overconfident. Often, people ask whether I am faking it, as in "Fake it until you make it." For me, the certainty of the Presence of the loving Creator is the same as knowing that no matter the storm's strength, even if it were to last for days on end, the sun would eventually reappear.

Up until the age of 40, I had believed that the source of my fearlessness had been external. I trusted there was an army of angels or the invisible hand of the Creator ready to come to my rescue at any moment's notice. In the past 10 years, spiritual teachers like Teilhard de Chardin (1) have made me realize that the source of my faith—that certainty that I can overcome anything—is internal. One of the teachings of de Chardin that resonates with me is "*En pasi panta theos*;" that God may be all in all. That is, through His/

Her/Its omnipresence, God is not just surrounding me; She resides within every tissue, every cell, every molecule, every atom, and subatomic particle of my being... meaning that at any given time, I can tap into the Infinite power of our Creator.

Adolescence can feel lonely for anyone. There were certainly times when I wished I had a parent or older sibling in whom I could confide or together with whom I could plan things. Playing and replaying the internal tape loop of "I am a Lone Wolf" helped me resist the temptation of indulging feelings of loneliness. While I wasn't immune to those feelings then, I believe it was much easier for me than most to eliminate them. They felt like a flock of birds that would go over my head, but I would never allow them to nest there.

While I called myself a Lone Wolf, I understood that this did not mean I would ever be lonely. I saw life as being on a mission in some foreign land. And while you are undercover in this land like a covert operative, there are collaborators, technologies, and knowledge that can be made available to you at a moment's notice to help ensure the mission's success.

During my time in both Guadeloupe and Haiti—which is to say, through my K–12 education—other than my mother, I did not feel that any of the adults caring for me had any genuine concern about whether I succeeded or failed. Whether I succeeded or not was *my* problem. In fairness, they probably had no idea about the best possible path for me, nor did they try to find out. I could probably have dealt with the lack of support regarding my education, but what was missing for me more than anything was the lack of emotional support. It is not that I was constantly craving for (or even seeking) it; but some acknowledgment, guidance, and validation—with just a little bit of love and care—would have gone a long way.

The love and care I was craving at home came from the blessing of having excellent teachers who took me under their wings. There is a verse in the great book that says, "God is for us a refuge, a rescue that never fails during difficult times" (Psalm 46:1). Those of us who have gone through challenging times know that this help and rescue comes in the form of the right people coming into our lives at the right time.

One of those people was my middle school teacher, Mrs. Botino. She was about the same age as my mother. Mrs. Botino was so sweet, and if she needed to be stern, she still delivered the message with a lot of love. On the academic side, I am grateful to her for encouraging me to take on Latin before I went to high school. I believe taking Latin was very helpful for building my university-level vocabulary, which allowed me to navigate higher education in America with almost as much ease as a native speaker.

More important than academic knowledge was an instance of pure, selfless love that I experienced in my interaction with Mrs. Botino. During my time there, we had to take two foreign languages before high school, with a third being possible but optional). I had selected English and Spanish as my two mandatory languages.

When it came to selecting a third, in response to Mrs. Botino's nudging to take Latin, I told her about my concerns that it was a dead language and it might not be as useful to me as taking something like German or Italian. Mrs. Botino responded, "As long as there are students like you taking Latin, it will never be a dead language." This affirmation of love and support meant a lot to me and went straight to my heart.

Another interaction with Mrs. Botino that remains etched in my memory occurred outside of school. It was in 1986 when we had just started seeing landlines appearing in households like ours. The public utility company, *Électricité de France* (EDF), had recently installed a landline phone in our house, and one afternoon, Mrs. Botino called me about some matter I no longer recall but wasn't that important. I believe I was just coming from a nap when she called, and I was the only one home at the time. I lifted the receiver, and the first words that came out of my mouth were, "Who is it?"

Mrs. Botino gently scolded me and told me that I needed to work on my phone etiquette. She gave me instructions on the types of greetings I could use.

Along with Mrs. Botino, several other teachers took an interest in me and provided support beyond their appointed duties. One such teacher was Mr. Bergeron, who pushed me further and admonished me when necessary. He invited me to his home several times and even gave me two small cats from one of his litters. Unfortunately, my home environment wasn't prepared to handle any domestic animals. One of the two cats ended up dying early, and I had to give the other away.

After the first year in high school, we had to choose a literary, economic, or scientific subject area; I was undecided between a literary or scientific track, as I was good in both. My French teacher took me aside and said, "I know you are a good writer. You can always write, no matter what career you select. However, if you don't do science, you can never come back to it. Many kids would like to go on the science track, but they don't have your skill level."

This was the best career advice I ever received. Going through the scientific route was less crowded indeed and opened many doors for me that I doubt would have been available otherwise.

The other way the Universe's support manifested was through books that came to my awareness at the right time. There are two books I stumbled upon that gave me more than academic knowledge. The curious part of this is that neither of them was part of my required reading at school, and hence, it is highly unlikely that I would have come across them if it were not for the fact that I was a library rat. Even with my frequent library visits, I believe the timing of their discovery was only attributable to divine intervention.

One of these two books is a work of fiction titled *La petite Fadette* ("*Little Fadette*") by the French author Georges Sand (2), whose real name was Amantine Lucile Aurore Dupin. I must have been attracted by the author's fierce spirit of independence—something I learned about after researching her when I'd finished the book. She would wear male attire and was known to smoke cigars in public, which women were forbidden to do at the time.

Little Fadette tells the story of a young girl from a humble family who has plain features and is misunderstood. I realized that I shared many similarities with Fanchon, the protagonist; along with her, I had the same sense of being perceived as not belonging and being "the odd man out." The book gave me conviction and comfort in being able to trust that, in the end, inner beauty is, in and of itself, sufficient to allow us to prevail in making our way through the world.

The novel's theme was deeply pertinent, as this was the critical period of my youth when I was experiencing being different—and being looked down upon by my peers. Although my classmates looked like me ("blacks" and descendants of slaves brought from Africa by the French) and spoke the same language as I (who was well versed in the French and the Guadeloupean local flavor of Creole), I was always perceived as an outsider due to my having been born in Haiti, which I never concealed from anyone and wore rather proudly.

Like Fanchon, I was also marginalized because of my social status. When I went into high school, the disparities between rich and poor became more evident. Up to my junior high school (during which time I was at the bottom of the social ladder), in comparison to my counterparts, our economic differences were not seen as being all that pronounced because our clothes were not that different. The school provided all our books, and we came from nearby neighborhoods.

By contrast, at the high school in Guadeloupe that I attended (*Lycée Polyvalent de Baimbridge),* the student population came from nearly half of the island. My schoolmates included students whose parents could afford to buy them cars that were often nicer than our teachers.

With this more diverse student population, the lack of quality in my clothing and shoes became more noticeable. While in high school, I was able to afford sneakers for physical education with money from side hustles such as tutoring, they stood out for their lack of branding and simplicity. Until high school, it wasn't always the case that I even *had* sneakers with which to attend Physical Education. I had to stoically fight off any shame to wear my *micas*—a closed sandal made with sturdy but flexible plastic. If the message that one needed to broadcast was, "I'm poor," then the wearing of *micas* would have been the biggest font one could have used to scream that message in the boldest of letters.

Despite my clothing being decent enough, I am sure that during my adolescence, I wasn't projecting any sense of external beauty into the world. I had fully embraced that I wasn't someone pleasing to the eye and that some even saw me as ugly. What I had going for me was my intellect and the ideals to which I tenaciously clung. Even in junior high, I had a strong reputation for advocating for social justice and what is right based on utilitarian principles. I often joked with my classmates, "I prefer to be a good book with a worn cover than an average book with a fancy cover."

La petite Fadette was an affirmation that I was okay—that I was enough and that I *had* enough. My inner attractiveness, which I was privately assured, was enough to enable me to conquer the world.

Another book I discovered when I was 16, which was (and continues to be) motivational for me, was *Meditations* by the emperor Marcus Aurelius (3). It was refreshing to find a soul in complete harmony with my thoughts, although our lives were separated by some two thousand years. The words resonated with me. It was as if Marcus Aurelius was repeating truths that I had buried deep within my soul, having been intimidated by their beauty and power.

In Aurelius' *Meditations,* it is almost as if you have a father giving you advice from beyond the grave, affirming your sensibilities and way of being. The book's teachings solidified my conviction that no matter how dire my external circumstances were, they did not define me and that it was okay to take a detached approach to events over which I had no control. This was the full permission I needed from the Universe to let my inner compass rule my world and not give in to emotions of despair or allow my environment to dictate who I am, how I should feel, or what my future should be.

This message of enlightened stoicism was needed and timely for a teenager who dared to dream big dreams of climbing to the highest echelons of education and building a business empire. Some saw me as a dangerous dreamer; others saw me as reckless as Icarus, who, in his ambitious aspirations to explore, flew too close to the sun and tragically fell to his death.

Before I could go on to build castles born of my dreams, however, I first needed to finish high school. In Guadeloupe (under the administration of the French), this meant passing rigorous testing that would decide whether one proceeds to pursue a higher education or is condemned to enact some form of menial work, as is customary in the very hierarchical French system. Getting a high school diploma was no guarantee of certainty—and at the time, the rate of failure was between 30% and 50%. In some schools, the failure rate was even higher, meaning less than half of the students would attain a high school diploma. One of the teachers who took me under his wing told me:

"You at least need to receive your baccalaureate to be considered of intellectual promise."

In 1989, I *did* succeed in receiving my baccalaureate, with a specialization in Mathematics and Sciences. I was ready to take on the world. The Universe had sent help when I needed it, enabling The Lone Wolf to achieve this milestone. My eyes were set on going to the equivalent of an MBA program, which required two years of preparatory school (*classes préparatoires*) to pass an exam for admission. I had the option of staying in Guadeloupe or going to

France for the prep programs—but something entirely out of the blue was about to derail my plans.

References for Chapter 4:

1. Teilhard de Chardin, P. (1960). *The divine milieu* (B. Wall, Trans.). Harper & Row. (Original work published 1957)

2. Sand, G (2020). "The Little Fadette". Hawthorne Classic [Note that when I read the book in my youth, it was the original French version]

3. Aurelius, M. (1997). *Meditations* (G. Long, Trans.). Dover Publications. (Original work published ca. 180)

CHAPTER 5

The Lone Wolf Pursues His Dreams (1989–1994)

*"Every great dream begins with a dreamer. Always remember,
you have within you the strength, the patience, and the
passion to reach for the stars to change the world."*

— Harriet Tubman

"Ou pa ka fè sa!"
("You cannot do this!")
"Tout sakrifis sa...!"
("All this sacrifice...!")

These were among the many unsolicited pieces of advice I repeatedly heard from family members. It was 1989, and I passed the exam, which enabled me to receive my high school diploma. While I knew that *Manman* had been working on getting me to the United States when I graduated, I had lost interest in going to America, with my eyes set instead on going to France. Why risk pursuing my education in a foreign language and an unknown setting?

Many of my friends in Guadeloupe saw my ambitions as a huge gamble. They reminded me of the racism in the US and that I was likely going to end up living in a ghetto as a second-class citizen, with the "Great American Dream" of worldly success and affluence still well beyond my reach. In one of those conversations with a classmate who was going to France, he lamented: "There is structural racism in France. For example, the French government would never send a Black prefect in Guadeloupe, but at

55

least you can get admitted to a Grande École de Commerce—one of the top schools for a master's in business administration in France."

The fear reflected here is that I might not even get a decent education in the US.

Another old-time friend from our church joked that: "Soon, you are going to eat a lot of hamburgers and have a big belly like an American."

This was as if becoming obese was the only certainty in my fate.

Being unable to pursue my education was the most concerning risk in investing in such a significant move. In France, I could see a path forward, whereas in the US, I had no firm idea of how solid the glass ceiling might be and how I could break through it. Even though France was not free of its pedigree of racism, at least I could count on access to education based on merit.

I understood there were certain systemic inequities in the United States, as well as in France, that were created and maintained by the dominant racial group. My preference for the French system was due to my confidence in the ideals underpinning their social system, such as "equality" and "fraternity,"—principles which I believed imposed a limit on how much discrimination would be tolerated.

After many proddings, beseechings, and sometimes guilt-making harangues on my sister's part, I gave in to the pressure from my family and decided to risk my luck in the New World.

In the summer of 1989, at 19, I arrived in America, landing at JFK, where I went through a lengthy immigration process since I was coming on an immigrant visa. Upon stepping outside, I first noticed the unending stream of yellow taxi cabs. I didn't have time to take in the extended surroundings, as I was bent on getting to my mother as soon as possible.

Manman had given me her address as 1402 Pitkin Avenue, Brooklyn, New York, and had told me that her boyfriend, Bertoni, would be awaiting me there. Given the number of Haitians in the taxi business in Brooklyn then, it was no coincidence that my taxi driver turned out to be a Haitian. I gave him the address, and when we arrived, he waited for me to get the fare money from Bertoni.

Although I know *Manman* trusted me to find my way from the airport, as someone who is *écléré* ("intellectual") as well as *débouya* ("enterprising"), I eventually concluded that the actual reason she hadn't come to the airport was that she couldn't afford to take a day off from work.

This was one of the first lessons I learned from my mother, as well as from the other immigrants in my community. You didn't take time off work just like that; you showed up for work no matter what. I've seen *Manman* suffering, cold and weak, and still summoning all her available strength to show up for work—even on the worst winter days. A typical sentence I would hear frequently from her was:

"In this country, you have to take your job seriously."

"Nan péyi sa, moun pa jwé a on moso travay non."

This dedication to work wasn't about any incentive for advancement or higher income; the overriding factor was to, in no case, risk losing your job and the income with which you needed to pay your bills.

There was also a herd mentality in *Manman* and the older immigrants of her generation. This mindset simply believed this was how American society worked, even though it may not have been quite what the Founding Fathers had envisioned in the right to pursue happiness bestowed upon all of us by our Creator. *Manman* believed that you were expected to show up for work and give it your best, whether you cherished that work or not.

The neighborhood *Manman* lived in was overwhelmingly black, with most of its residents hailing from Jamaica and Haiti, along with a few Latinos here and there. It was a typical Brooklyn neighborhood, with brick row houses all in a line, broken up by an occasional grocery store. Our local store was the size of a large bed-room owned by Dominican Republic immigrants.

A few blocks from our house, along Pitkin Avenue, there was a commercial district where you could find a furniture store owned by a Haitian businessman. I remember it well: "*Mézi* furniture" ("*Mézi*" being any kind of furniture that you might need). It's hard to forget this establishment; they ran endless commercials on Haitian media at the time. "*Gadé on Mézi, Ou konin'm sézi.*" ("*Wow, look at all this furniture, I'm really surprised.*"). Sadly, the proprietor of *Mézi* was killed in one of the frequent but senseless robbery attempts around this time.

Upon my arrival in Brooklyn, one of the first things I became aware of was the prevalence—indeed, the sheer persistence—of crime, and the consequent need to be especially vigilant about one's safety. Our neighborhood was one of the worst; I was told that a couple of blocks beyond our house was a no-go zone for the New York City Police and that after sunset, they would not even bother to respond to a call.

Whether this was true or not, I would never have an opportunity to find out. I stayed in Brooklyn for 18 months before we moved to New Jersey, and in that time, I never once ventured even a single block past our house at night in the direction of the business district on Pitkin Avenue.

As for our safety, *Manman* and my brother Jonas (who had come to the States before me) had tutored me on how to protect myself:

"Never go onto the last subway car."

"Make sure you are in a subway car with many people..."

"When you leave the station, walk briskly."

And:

"Always be on the lookout and check your surroundings."

But none of these precautions kept me out of reach of the crime wave that was so prevalent then. One night, coming from work around 11:00 p.m., as I was going up the stairs exiting the Eastern Parkway subway station near our home, a group of young men pretending to have a casual conversation ambushed me and started throwing punches. I was lucky that even though I got hit by one of them, I was able to escape to safety.

The second time, I wasn't so lucky; I was leaving the same subway station when a group of men surrounded me out of nowhere before I could leave the platform. They started hitting me until I fell, then they took my wallet and ran off.

In many island cultures, there is an underlying sense of unity emerging out of shared cultural and familial root systems, creating a world in which no one ever truly feels themselves to be an underling or an outlier; hence, even while at times one finds themselves experiencing loneliness, they are never tempted to truly feel like an outlier or an underling, alone and unsupported.

Not so, however, with "The Great Society"… instead, there is a feeling of exposure, vulnerability, and risk from myriad threats coming at one from many different directions—creating a kind of existential paranoia, as it were.

And so, apart from a few supportive family members (my closest brother Jonas, in particular), I found myself flying solo and subsisting through my own devices far more than I had ever anticipated. At this juncture in my life, even my relationship with *Manman* had become far more distant, with little in the way of the human or spiritual nurture it had once provided.

To be clear, when I arrived in America, it wasn't only as bad as I thought it would be—it was worse. Physical security wasn't my only concern; it was clear to me that working in the US wasn't just important… it was critical and part of one's identity. If you didn't work, you were a bum—a societal outcast.

To my silent shock, one of the first "conscious" conversations Manman took pains to have with me was not about my college plans—but rather about work. It must have been as early as the first week I was in America that she took me aside to explain to me how things worked:

"*Pitit mwen* ('my son'), bills must be paid in America. There is electricity, water, telephone (the time of landlines) and cable. Everyone has to pay for where they are staying and share in the bills. The good news is that in America, everyone can find a job. Even high school students work to help their families."

I "got" the message loud and clear: I was expected to get a job to help—and the sooner, the better. But anyone who knows me would have already known it's not in my nature to depend on anyone for my subsistence, for the idea of being a parasite horrifies me. I didn't enjoy those probing conversations, always questioning whether or not I had found something.

In no time, I had mastered the New York City subway system. I wasn't just waiting on people to give me job leads; I was buying newspapers like *The New York Times* and the *Daily News* and venturing into Manhattan to go door to door to restaurants, bookstores, and retail stores to find something—anything—that would bring some money in. Given that I had come too late to attend university in the fall of 1989, my first thought was to make some money instead of attending college. Still, I was looking for something that would allow me to transition to school part-time once I had begun working.

But my efforts were in vain. After many failed searches, I decided to try McDonalds, where I was told anyone could get a job. And I did. On my first day, however, I realized there was no way I could do such mindless work with the added stresses of the heat, the pace, and the overall job environment. I knew I just couldn't do it. I quit after that first day and never returned.

The second job I obtained was with UPS, loading and unloading boxes, requiring me to start or end work at 3:00 a.m. Despite the insecurity and crime in Brooklyn, the decent pay lured me, and

I was determined to take it. Friends of the family begged me to do otherwise, and in the end, I relented.

The frustration of being unable to find a job was one of many factors that caused me to despair in my new homeland. This is the first time in my life where I felt so trapped without knowing when the situation would change or whether my efforts would eventually be successful. One night, I cried like a baby over the life I was living—a life that had been selected for me but held no promise of achieving my life goals.

Aside from not working, my living conditions could have been better. We were living in a one-bedroom apartment on the ground floor of our building. When first entering the unit, there was a living room area where my brothers (Jonas and Stanley) and I slept on a full-size sofa bed and a full-size bed. *Manman* and Berthony shared the bedroom in the middle of the unit. At the end of the unit was the kitchen area, which harbored an imposing closet. However, that closet was not a pantry; it contained merchandise *Manman* was selling to supplement her income.

Living in a one-bedroom apartment with four other people felt like living in a shoebox. The living room before we arrived was like many Haitian households that I had visited: clogged with too much bric-a-brac that, while decorative, looked cheap and might better have been given away. This included a lot of porcelain-like figurines called *biblo*, odd furniture to feature them on, and what seemed to be a ubiquitous wall tapestry depicting the Last Supper. It was as if there were some sort of compulsion to acquire things—things that weren't needed but which one liked or had glimpsed at other Haitian homes.

The level of segregation in America shocked me; of course, I had heard about it, and had read a couple of books by the black, native-born American writer James Baldwin, but the degree and extent of it was beyond my imagination.

Our neighborhood was pervasively covered with broken glass, and I never saw police officers routinely patrolling our block. This was quite the reverse to the Jewish neighborhoods just a 10-minute walk from us, which were clean, quiet, and well-patrolled. I understood that the Jewish community had more political influence and could demand more public services through their connections with the mayor's office.

As far as Manhattan goes, except perhaps for Harlem, living there was financially out of reach. The dramatic contrast between the city and the neighborhood we lived in made it seem like we were traveling between two totally different countries, even though they were only separated by a bridge and lay less than an hour's subway ride.

In Manhattan, there was no need for someone to tell you that you didn't belong; it was visible in how they looked at you—or rather, didn't even bother to look at you. In the early days, before I knew that New Yorkers didn't talk to strangers (at least at that time), I went to ask someone for directions, and they simply ignored me. No eye contact whatsoever... no words... I simply did not exist. I would later learn to preface such mundane interactions with the words, "I'm not asking for money..."

I also happened to arrive in the city at a time of heightened racial tensions, which very probably made the issue of segregation look even worse. One such incident I remember well happened within a month of my arrival in the city. A young black man named Yusuf Hawkins had been murdered by a mob of youths in an Italian neighborhood because they thought he was dating "one of their girls."

While I would eagerly admit that the racial tensions were not as extreme as they seemed to be, they were undoubtedly greatly amplified by the segregation of cultures into mutually exclusive neighborhoods. I wondered what kind of a world I had placed myself into.

There was a cauldron of unvoiced fury raging within me, which I was only marginally able to harness through the dual moral directives of my Haitian-Christian upbringing.

I confess that a part of me was angry not just at the trying living conditions in America but also at my mother. I felt that my only reason for being in America was to help her pay her bills. I'm not sure she ever grasped that my saying "no" to the temptation of obtaining a green card and focusing on studying at one of the French academic institutions I had been accepted into would have been better for me.

Despite love and mutual admiration, many years apart had created a gap, which was perhaps unavoidable (or at least predictable) between us. The gap in question was more cultural than the typical age-related tensions I imagine must plague every generation of human societies. These cultural tensions are about the expectations parents have of their children.

There is a common saying in Haitian society that illustrates this idea:

"A donkey has younglings so its back can take a break."

"Bourik fè pitit sé pou do l pozé."

This rebellious part of me felt like I had not signed up for this, and I shouldn't have to bankrupt my future for anyone—especially when I had asked (or been the recipient of) so little.

Although I was frustrated about where my life was going, I could simultaneously appreciate *Manman's* position, which I could readily empathize with.

She had fought to leave Haiti for Guadeloupe to offer my siblings and me the chance for better education, moved to the US, and did everything she could to get us into the country legally. Against all odds, she had saved as much money as she could to get us to America—the "promised land," in her eyes—so that we would have a chance to achieve the American Dream and become a *gran neg* ("rich negro"). And she was expecting us to show appreciation for what she had accomplished.

About our green cards, *Manman* would sometimes say:

"This piece of paper you have in your hands, some people are looking for it in Heaven; you found it on the ground, and you are not appreciating it."

One of the harrowing feelings that enveloped me during that time was the fear of being trapped in a virtual prison—which is to say, living in a society where I was limited as to what I could do with my life. To me, this would have been a fate worse than death.

What triggered my misgivings more than anything else was meeting many well-educated immigrants who had taken menial jobs to make ends meet. I knew of individuals who had been university professors, engineers, agronomists, and journalists in Haiti who, unable to find work in their professions, had to settle for driving taxis.

Back then, climbing the ladder and owning your taxi medallion (controlled by the City Taxi and Limousine Service, which conferred upon you the right to own a taxi) was a coveted possession. But, at a price of tens of thousands of dollars, it was a life-consuming achievement in and of itself.

I also met fellow Haitians who had settled for blue collar union jobs or government work with great benefits and decent pay. Many of these individuals had arrived in New York City but needed to pursue more education or dedicate time to learning enough English. These were often sucked into the vortex of American life and the struggle to make ends meet, even if it meant sacrificing one's soul to do so, never knowing when (or if) you might ever have another chance to escape such a Devil's Bargain—just so long as it paid the bills. No wonder I was afraid of losing myself in the jaws of that soul-sucking machinery.

Eventually, after much perseverance, I found a decent, stable job at Barnes & Noble in Lower Manhattan. What seemed like an eternity had had only been three months at most, as I had secured the job before the coming of the fall months imposed the spell of darkness upon us.

With this job in hand, I could pay my fair share of the bills and move on to the next challenge—pursuing an education. In this effort, I found encouragement and support from other young Haitian immigrants who preceded me. Several people at church educated me about the possibilities for financial aid, as well as the details of the application process.

One of those individuals was my cousin Wayne, who emigrated in 1975. When I told him about my concerns about having to compete in English against native speakers, he shut my fearmongering down. His words were:

"You are going to be competing against kids from Iowa or the ghettos, where the education is substandard, whereas you have received a world-class education in the French system. These students can't compete with you."

The support I received from my Haitian peers and my diligent efforts allowed me to enroll at Baruch College, a branch of the City University of New York (CUNY), in January 1990. Even with the delay caused by my move to America, I managed to miss only one semester.

Her children being in America gave my mother the big break she had hoped for because my brother Jonas and I helped pay the bills, and she could now save more of her own money. This was also when students like me, with limited financial contributions from their parents, could receive state and federal funding toward their living costs beyond merely tuition and books.

By the end of 1990, I gave my mother an additional $3,000 to add to her savings for a down payment on a house in Trenton, New Jersey, in early 1991. However, moving out of New York City was not something I was looking forward to.

At that time, I was hitting my stride; I had a part-time job, had found a good church community while also remaining close to my extended family, and I was on track to obtain my ticket to the American Dream—a college education. One of my cousins had succeeded in escaping the city's busy hustle and crime-ridden streets, and *Manman* was bent on following her example.

Manman and I were not on the same page regarding education and getting a bachelor's degree as soon as possible. For her, the American Dream was having a house she could call her own—just like her sister, my Aunt Andrée, who had sponsored her to come to America.

Did this mean that I would have to give up continuing my education?

Our move to Trenton only required me to take the fall semester of 1991 off. By the spring of 1992, I had transferred to Rutgers University and was commuting about an hour per trip to New Brunswick from Trenton to resume my studies. However, living on campus was simply not an option; while I could have afforded it with the help of government grants and my part-time work, I also knew Manman depended on my contribution to the mortgage.

Even with all these setbacks, however, I was able, by December 1993, to achieve what was (for me) the classic cornerstone of the American Dream—a college degree. At the time, Rutgers only awarded degrees in the spring semester, so I had to wait until May to receive my diploma.

Several factors contributed to the speed with which I reached this milestone. Because I had received 12 credits for my French baccalaureate from Baruch College, I had already completed the equivalent of a semester from the get-go. I also took on a heavy course load despite working part-time and spending two hours daily commuting.

This included a semester where I took on a load of 21 credits. During that semester, unfortunately, I had a major accident—the result of falling asleep at the wheel in the early commute to my part-time job that started at 7:00 a.m. after a long night of studying. The car was totaled, and I spent a week in the hospital.

Miraculously, however, my injuries turned out to be superficial! It was a miracle, and it was certainly no less impressive than the many too-close-for-comfort calls that had occurred during my trips back and forth between Trenton and New Brunswick, in which I felt that my life had been spared at the very last moment.

I recalled one "close call" moment when I completely blanked out and crossed a red light on the busy Highway Route 1 in Princeton. The many times I fell asleep at a stoplight or stop sign, only to be awakened by an impatient driver behind me, were too numerous to count.

Against all odds, and with what I strongly feel to have been protection from one or many invisible hands, I had overcome what I considered the biggest obstacle—being college-educated.

In the wake of this heady achievement, I was filled with invincibility... I was ready to take on the world.

From then on, I felt the wind would be at my back.

Why not? What could stop me? I was led to believe that when you graduated from a good school with decent grades, you would have no problem finding a good-paying job. So, I was nearly salivating at the prospect of finally having a nice paycheck that would allow me to save money before undertaking graduate studies.

In April 1994, with the degree not yet in hand but all my requirements completed, I felt confident enough about my job prospects to ask my then-girlfriend Valery to marry me. She was a longtime family friend, and I had met her mother (who connected us) while living in Guadeloupe. Our engagement was short, and we married in July that same year. Right after our marriage, we moved to the Raleigh-Durham area of North Carolina—an area recently named the most desirable American town to live in. It also happened to have one of the best graduate programs in statistics, one that I had my eyes set on in the future.

What could stop us? The answer was short in coming, as I would very soon discover further yet unsuspected rough patches on the road to the Great American Dream.

CHAPTER 6

The Hunt of the Lone Wolf: Corporate America (1994–2003)

"Machan chèché, pa janm domi san soupé"
"If you search long enough, you will not go to bed hungry."
— Haitian Proverb

We arrived in North Carolina at the end of July 1994 ("we" being Valery, myself, and our eight-year-old daughter Katina, who had come as a gift from the marriage). Somehow, although neither of us had jobs, we had managed to obtain a decent enough apartment in the western part of Raleigh, the capital city, with two bedrooms and one bathroom. While the state ranked at the bottom for education in 1994, Wake County (which Raleigh was a part of) ranked at the top nationally, and the west side of the town had even better schools.

By faith, or what someone else might call sheer naïveté, we had assumed it would be a simple matter for us to find employment.

However, were we in for a surprise!

Contrary to what I was told, a bachelor's degree did not guarantee getting a job. Despite churning resumes out like a paper mill, I couldn't find a "professional job"—which is to say, an office job where they would trust an ambitious college graduate. I would painstakingly take time to send personalized cover letters and tailor my resume to the specifics of the job description, but nothing worked.

In the end, we needed to generate income and pay the bills. To make ends meet, I took on a few odd jobs. Interestingly, one was at the SAS Institute and came through a temporary work agency. SAS Institute made software for analyzing data. While my degree was

69

in mathematics, I knew more than enough about statistics and programming to be accepted for an entry-level programmer job with the company. However, the best I could find at first was a job as a janitor working an early shift from 4:00 a.m. to noon, and then after that ended, another job with that same agency helping the landscaping crew.

What kept me going during these jobs at SAS was my faith that the Universe would eventually come through; all I had to do was my part—which was just to show up. Even though all that was available was cleaning bathrooms, I gave it my best. I woke up every morning knowing that the Universe was working on fulfilling my dream. I assumed something that would use my college degree would eventually open up, and that I would finally be on the inside track.

While going through this dark period, my spirit was high; several books helped me maintain this positivity. Two books still stand out are *Seeds of Greatness* by Denis Waitley and *Developing the Qualities of Success* by Zig Ziglar. These books encouraged me to keep my spirit up and give my best in the most menial jobs while at the same time not giving up on my dreams.

I worked at SAS for about four months, during which no professional job opportunity appeared. At this time, I had to take a second job at Circuit City (a former competitor of Best Buy, which has since disappeared) as a sales clerk in their Small Electronics Department.

Eventually, however, something finally opened up at SAS.

It was a permanent janitorial position. While this was not what I wanted, I would get a pay bump—and, more importantly, receive good benefits for my family and me. Given that I had done the job as a temp worker and given it my best, I felt I was sure to get it. I went to the Human Resources Department and filled out my application. I hesitated to list my college degree, but I knew I couldn't lie, so in the end, I simply noted that I had graduated from college.

The lady who took my application was a young female worker in her late twenties or early thirties. She glanced at my application, and our conversation collapsed my heart.

"I am not going to be able to recommend you for this position—you are too qualified," she told me.

I almost broke, but I stoically shared with her: "At this point, I don't care. I need a stable job with the benefits."

However, there was a comforting sense of care in her reply that was difficult for me to forget: "Don't give up," she told me. "You will waste your talent if you take on this job. Eventually, you will find the right position."

Indeed, a short time later, I *did* find a teaching position, which I would eventually leave to pursue graduate studies in the fall of 1995.

When I look back at my life, I am so grateful for all the unanswered prayers made simply to get any available job, just because I needed to put food on the table—jobs that might have been dead ends and soul-crushing.

I had concluded that to advance, I had to stick to my original plans to pursue graduate studies.

This was also a time of racial tension in North Carolina. In 1995, the state was gearing up for a tense election rematch between incumbent Senator Jesse Helms and Harvey Gantt, the former and first black Mayor of Charlotte, the largest city in the state. During this time, I became aware of an ad called "The White Hands," which had been used during the previous contest between them.

The ad showed a white woman in a kitchen with a voiceover saying something like:

"You wanted this job for your family, but they had to give it to a minority because of affirmative action."

After college, my original plan was to find a good-paying job that would still enable me to pursue my graduate studies part-time. However, the repeated job rejections I received and the racial context at the time in North Carolina convinced me to pursue graduate studies without delay, regardless of the consequences. I had determined that it wasn't enough for me to be good—I had to be excellent. I had to show up with such qualifications that I would not be refused a seat at the table.

With my teaching job at a private school bringing in barely enough to cover household expenses, the new plan was to pursue graduate school full-time and supplement my income with a part-time job. My program of study was statistics at North Carolina State University, one of the country's top programs at the time. This was when, if you pursued a doctoral degree in a field of sciences such as statistics, you would get some financial support from the program that provided enough funding for tuition and living expenses.

As soon as I was accepted into the graduate program in early March of 1995, we learned some exciting and frightening news: Valery had become pregnant.

Like any new parents—and particularly given that this was going to be our first "creation"—we were excited to bring someone new into this life who would become a part of us. How would this baby look? Which one of us would they look like the most? Would we be creating a "mini-me" for one of us? Whose eyes or hair color would that baby have? In imagining who the baby would look like the most, Valery would often say, "The baby can be a carbon copy for me; I hope that baby is smart enough to take the hair of their dad, definitely the brains, and if they're a boy, the eyes."

On the "brains" topic, we had a slight disagreement. I have always admired Valery's smartness. If you gave us problems that required quick thinking, that would be her domain. My strength is more for the issues that require grit and perseverance. Take language skills, for example; we both had the same levels of Spanish when we started our relationship. Over time, however, my proficiency in Spanish became better only because I was willing to take risks in engaging strangers and making mistakes. The baby would be fine if they received the brain gene from either of us. I also don't believe it's a matter of subjectivity to say that Valery is stunningly beautiful. So, in those conversations, I would joke: "Any baby of us, if they are brilliant, would pick their look from their mother."

While we were excited at the prospect of seeing the fruits of our marriage materializing in the form of a human being, we also had to consider the reality of having enough income to take care of an additional family member. To make matters worse, the pregnancy was difficult, and Valery eventually had to quit her full-time job, which brought much-needed income to cover our expenses.

While we didn't know how we would make it with only one person bringing in money, looking at all the options in front of us, we just knew that going to graduate school was the only choice and that we would figure it out from there.

Ultimately, despite some reservations and second-guessing whether it was right, I enrolled in the doctoral program at North Carolina State University in the Statistics Department. Although I knew then that I would leave to start making some decent money after earning a master's degree, a key advantage to enrolling as a doctoral student was getting financial support through a fellowship or as a teaching assistant. The fellowship would have been ideal since it required no work obligations. However, I was grateful to at least receive support through the teaching assistantship.

The first year of graduate school was, to say the least, demanding.

Intellectually, the courses were by far the most rigorous I had ever encountered, with extensive homework assignments that my classmates often tackled together in study groups. Unfortunately, due to my work commitments, I didn't have the luxury of joining them.

It wasn't just that I had a part-time job; I worked more than 40 hours a week during my first year of graduate school. Taking on so much work was a necessity for me if we were going to cover the expenses of our household. I took a full-time security position, in which I was working a second (and sometimes third) shift. The main advantage of that security job was that I could get some of my homework done.

Aside from that security position, I discovered a French School by browsing the Yellow Pages. This was when there were several French companies in the Raleigh-Durham area—particularly in the telecommunications industry, such as Alcatel. Because these French executives were temporarily stationed in North America, they needed a school that conformed to the French curriculum so their children could quickly re-integrate into the French national educational system when they returned home from the US.

During the summer of 1995 (at the end of which I had to take a qualifying exam), I realized there was no way I could pass the exam unless I devoted more time to studying. The dilemma was that if I were to stop working, we would have no income to pay our bills.

How, I wondered, was I going to solve this?

An Associate Dean at the University was responsible for supporting minority students in the sciences. I contacted him to see if his office could provide some financial support. This was a long shot, as I didn't know whether this had ever been done.

So, I asked for a meeting and poured my heart out regarding my situation.

"Dean," I told him, "I know I can pass this exam, but I need time to study for it. I have a family to feed, and I've been working more than while preparing for my qualifying exam. On the other hand, my classmates can spend the summer focusing entirely on the exam."

To my surprise, it went as well as I could have hoped. The Dean told me he would find funding for a supplemental scholarship. This was the quickest process I could imagine. In less than a week, I received notice of the award, which came in as a lump sum payment, allowing me to take care of some lingering bills and dedicate my time to studying for the qualifying exam.

While I didn't get a passing grade to continue to the PhD program, I *did* get a passing grade to obtain a master's degree. It was the same test used for both master's and doctoral programs, with the only difference being postgraduate students had to earn a higher passing grade.

Having passed my master's exam in the summer, I proceeded (in the fall semester of my second year of the program) to resume looking for a job. Unlike in the case of my bachelor's degree, the responses I received were very positive early on.

My first meaningful job interview happened in December, before the fall semester's close— before the semester itself was over. The company was Micron Technology, based out of Boise, Idaho. This interview was meaningful because I had a second, in-person interview for which they flew me in, paid for me to spend a few days there to see how I would feel, and gave me the freedom to look around the area for houses to buy if I were to accept their offer.

They made me an offer, which I turned down for several reasons. First, Boise didn't look that diverse to me. During the three days I spent there, I can't remember meeting even one soul with a skin complexion like mine. Second, I was afraid that if I wanted to switch employers at some point, I would be forced to relocate with one of the few employers in my field in Idaho. Finally, I couldn't ignore that despite the great weather when I arrived, the best winter days in Boise didn't compare well against even a bad one in North Carolina.

So, although I turned down this job, it was helpful (and perhaps providential) that it came first. After checking my references, the hiring manager called me. He began:

"I need to share something very confidential with you. I called one of your references, and they didn't give you a good recommendation. They mentioned that your performance is inconsistent. The quality of your work is not always on par with what you're capable of."

While I was disappointed to hear this, I was level with him.

"I can see where that professor is coming from," I said. "As I mentioned during the interview, unlike most of my peers, my life situation was such that I had to work full-time—and at times, well more than the required 40 hours a week—while simultaneously pursuing graduate school full-time. There were many periods when I could not invest as much time in my studies as I would have wished."

His response was conciliatory:

"I remember you saying that, and that's why I'm sharing this information with you. I had to work part-time while in school, and I know what it's like. Because of that, I appreciate what you've accomplished here."

From the information gleaned from that dialogue, I identified the person I believe to have been the culprit and eliminated them from my list of references in future job searches. Shortly after that, I had a second interview with a large employer in North Carolina called the Research Triangle Institute (now RTI International). This was early in the spring semester, and they made me an offer relatively quickly, including me starting part-time immediately.

As the sole wage earner in the household, I was compelled by a sense of urgency to find a new job. By now, we had two kids, with a third—my youngest son, Vijay—on the way and expected to arrive in May 1994 (just in time for my graduation). I had a couple of promising interviews with banks in North Carolina, one of which was coming with the title of Vice President. Even though I was aware there were so many people in banking with the title of VP that if you lay them side by side, you could circle the Earth several times, it *did* tickle a part of my ego to think that I had graduated into potential VP status.

The only problem with the RTI offer was the salary. However, with my family situation, I didn't have the luxury of waiting. With the old Haitian proverb *sak nan men ou, se li ki rélé ou pa ou* ("what you own is what you hold in your hands") ringing in my ears, I chose to take the RTI job.

My starting salary was only $36,000 a year. My office mate, with just a bachelor's degree, was making $32,000. The benefit I got from this first job that I might not have gotten in many other places was the opportunity to learn. It felt like I had learned more in my first five months in that position than during my entire master's program. I was given time to sharpen my programming skills to the point that I was called a "guru" when programming complex data management tasks. I also took classes to develop broader skills, such as writing reports and proposals.

Taking on every training offered on the job that could advance my career was only part of the equation. I raised my hands whenever there was a complex project or task my colleagues didn't want. For example, I took on a task that involved estimating drug use in all US counties and constructing a data set with an observation for every individual in the US population. In 1998, even with access to the most advanced computer system, such a large data set called for a lot of creativity to develop an optimal program that ran in minutes (rather than hours).

Another task I eagerly volunteered for was writing proposals. The ability to write winning proposals would serve me not just in my present job but also in my next one and in my first company, SciMetrika, LLC.

The long hours I poured in were rewarded in my first year with what might appear to be a significant bump. It brought my salary from $36K to $45K (roughly close to a 20% increase). Although underpaid, however meager this salary was for a family of five, it was nevertheless a middle-class family salary that enabled us to move from our two-bedroom apartment to a three-bedroom house with a one-car garage in one of those sprawling subdivisions that contained both starter homes for families like us and (within that same subdivision) larger units for families with higher incomes.

After nine years of being in America, this was the first victory for the Lone Wolf. I had climbed what was, in my mind, the first ladder of the American dream—buying a home in the suburbs.

Based on percentage, while the increase I received at RTI was perhaps the largest in my unit (or even across the organization), I realized I had started so low that it would take me too long to be on par regarding salary. I had no illusion of the unlikelihood of RTI continuing to grant me these types of raises forever.

With the reality of being underpaid and the probability that I would not continue to be rewarded for my efforts year after year, I left RTI. I switched to a smaller, more entrepreneurial company with about $15 million in revenues. With that shift alone, my salary jumped from $45K to $60K (an increase of some 30%). The company in question was called Analytical Sciences, Inc., which would later change its name to Constella Group (Constella).

Constella was the epitome of what you would call an "entrepreneurial organization." The company had aggressive goals for growth and rewarded those who contributed to that growth. Year after year, I received double-digit salary increases with annual bonuses.

Throughout this period, I focused on advancing my career, investing time in learning as much as possible and being more productive than anyone. My *modus operandi* then was that although I might sometimes be outsmarted, I would never be outworked. This meant burning the midnight oil, arriving early, and leaving late (or being the last soul to leave our office the day before Thanksgiving).

My efforts were not just rewarded with salary increases. I was also constantly promoted, starting as a contributing and advancing to senior statistician; then project manager, responsible for overseeing a component task within a more extensive project; then rising to the position of project manager overseeing multiple components; and then finally, to program manager overseeing a portfolio of projects.

In my role as a program manager, I was responsible for the delivery of work to clients and also for winning more projects.

One year (in 2002), I had achieved a success rate of 100% on proposals I had pursued. Several of my colleagues approached me and told me:

"If you can win so many proposals independently, you should open your own company."

Consequently, I approached my boss (with whom I had an open and transparent relationship) and told him I was considering opening my own business.

His candid response was:

"You have been so successful because you have the name of the company behind you. You would never have been able to win these contracts without the company's brand behind you."

What I heard from this conversation was:

"The only reason you have been so successful is because you are part of a franchise. You must accept the need to pay the franchise fee and receive the crumbs from any money you're instrumental in bringing in because that is only made possible by the brand's reputation."

What the voice of my alter ego, the Lone Wolf, was telling me in the background was:

"Your boss is telling you that you are a franchisee of the company. If you go out on your own and hang a shingle with your brand, although you might win fewer contracts, you can keep more earnings."

So, in 2003, I started going after contracts set aside for small businesses that were too small for my employer to pursue. I secured a few small contracts that I could do by myself or with the part-time help of subcontractors. In 2004, I won a contract large enough to enable me to leave my job and start my entrepreneurial journey full-time.

After five years with Constella, I had climbed one more rung of the ladder of the American dream—success in corporate America. I had a secure job at which I excelled and had no worries. But more than just job security, I achieved *employment* security; I could go anywhere and find a new job.

⊷— —⊷

They say you can't make an omelet without breaking an egg. Climbing the corporate ladder came at a cost, not just for me but for my family. Long hours at the office meant fewer moments playing lawn games after work or teaching my children how to ride a bike. Often overlooked is the unique challenge fathers face: society's dual expectation of being the steadfast "breadwinner" without sacrificing time with their children.

Still, I found fulfillment in knowing that my hard work provided opportunities for my children that might have otherwise been out of reach. These included sports and summer camps, activities that enriched their experiences and supported their dreams. Katina and our youngest daughter, Valexa, both pursued gymnastics, inspired in part by the accomplishments of Dominique Dawes, an African-American gymnast who defied expectations with her visible strength and resilience. Katina admired her and often said, "You can have strong bones and still be a good gymnast." Starting gymnastics later than her peers meant Katina faced a steep learning curve, which limited her competitiveness. By contrast, Valexa started young and had an innate drive that propelled her to a level that could have opened doors for college-level competition. However, I was happy when she chose to step back during high school to focus on her studies.

I made it a point never to miss my children's piano recitals or competitions, even when gymnastics meets required full-day commitments or overnight stays. While these activities may seem routine for many suburban families, for me, they represented a tangible piece of the American dream. It wasn't just about providing; it was about giving my children the experiences that would inspire them and level the playing field for their futures.

I committed to playing just as hard to compensate for the time spent working so many long hours. Thankfully, Valery embraced this philosophy with me. Since our marriage, we prioritized vacations even when we had very little. Our first getaway, just a year into our marriage, was a modest weekend on the North Carolina coast, staying in an affordable spot in Wilmington, 30 minutes from the beach. As we progressed in our careers, our vacations improved from off-season stays near the water to week-long beachfront rentals in places like Myrtle Beach, South Carolina.

In 2004, I left the comfort of a corporate job to start my own business, which I'll delve into in the next chapter. The business's success allowed us to create even richer memories through international travel, cruises, and events such as professional sports games. One of the most satisfying ways I express love is through the gift of time. I am grateful to have shared memorable experiences, like attending the rare instances when the Haitian men's national soccer team advanced past the qualifying rounds of the CONCACAF tournament. I cherished those times—once with Valery in Texas and another with my son Vladimir, watching Haiti play Brazil. I was also fortunate to take a one-day trip with my daughter Valexa to see the original cast of *Hamilton* in New York City.

CHAPTER 7

Beneath the Mask
(2004–2013)

*"You wander from room to room hunting for the
diamond necklace that is already around your neck."*

— Rumi

The professional growth I had achieved at Constella Group allowed me to leave corporate America in 2004 and pursue my long-time dream of becoming a full-time entrepreneur. This was possible because I had won a small business set-aside contract with the US Department of Veteran Health Administration (VHA), which provided me with a reliable salary for the next two years.

Winning that contract would provide the momentum for my first company, SciMetrika, LLC (which I ran until selling it in 2018). The company is still in existence under its new ownership.

The aim for SciMetrika was to partner with government health agencies to offer science-based and methodology-driven solutions. While I was with my previous employer, Constella, I noticed that the contract service industry for public health services was very fragmented in the US. Unlike the defense industry (with such behemoths as Lockheed, Grumman, and Boeing), there were no major public health-oriented firms in 2004 when I started SciMetrika.

Why leave a good-paying job like I had while being the sole wage earner supporting your family?

I had always dreamed of becoming an entrepreneur. My first foray into entrepreneurship was in Guadeloupe when I was 11 years old and had convinced my mother to buy me two chicks with which (in my childhood dream) I would build a large chicken business. Even as a kid, my dreams were never small.

This dream continued in my teenage years and was cemented by watching a TV series called *Dallas*. There is something I found mesmerizing about the "wheeling and dealing" lifestyle of the protagonists, the Ewing Family. While I certainly would not condone the tactics used by the characters in that series to achieve business at all costs, something about their pursuit of success appealed to me.

It is not every childhood or teenage dream that we pursue. We grow out of some of these dreams. Having young mouths to feed at home is usually enough for most of us to shelve any youthful desires that could affect our ability to put food on the table predictably.

Starting a business was so ingrained that I felt it would keep me unfulfilled if I didn't pursue that path because I had seen many friends with good-paying jobs become shackled with the proverbial "golden handcuffs." They had jobs that enabled them to maintain a lifestyle where they could afford a lot of toys and take lavish vacations. At the same time, however, they were miserable in these jobs and felt they had reached a dead end where they would never advance.

One such former friend who worked for IBM and had an MBA from Duke confided in me:

"I thought that with my background in engineering and an MBA from a top program like Duke, I would be on track to become a top executive. Instead, I see young professionals I have trained getting ahead of me."

Thus, at 34, with my youngest child only four years old, waiting for my kids to be in college or out of the house was not an option I was willing to explore. I wanted to act before I got too comfortable.

The timing for me to quit was also optimal because I was painfully aware as a young Black man that there was likely to be a ceiling in my professional trajectory. I sensed that I was getting close to that when there was a layer of management added between my then-supervisor and me.

Beyond these external factors and the timing involved, my strongest motivation was the desire to control my destiny. I needed to take complete charge of my professional career, and the only way to ensure I would reach my goals was to be at the steering wheel.

There was this inner dialogue happening in me:

"What is the chance that a young Black man with a foreign accent in the middle of Dixie (although I was in what was called the "New South") would get a seat at the executive table?"

Given that I was unlikely to be invited into the room where the big decisions were made, the only choice I saw was to build my own.

After some early challenges, SciMetrika grew rapidly. Between 2007 and 2011, we doubled every year—and even tripled revenue in one of these years.

Our success at SciMetrika was recognized through several awards. In 2011 and 2012, we won the Inc Magazine 500 as one of the fastest-growing companies in America. Naturally, the national recognition translated into regional awards as well. Between 2008 and 2012, we made the list of the 50 fastest-growing companies for four years in a row, culminating in us being the number-two company with the fastest growth in 2012.

While SciMetrika was growing exponentially, I was pursuing another very dear goal: obtaining my doctorate.

In 1999, at the encouragement of my supervisor and mentor at Constella, I enrolled part-time in the doctoral program in the Department of Biostatistics at the University of North Carolina. By the time I started SciMetrika, I had completed all the coursework and was working on my dissertation.

Completing classes for a doctoral program was not any more complicated than doing so for a bachelor's or master's degree. The outcome for completing any doctoral level class was never in doubt. Overall, I found my master's level classes far more intellectually challenging than those for my doctoral degree. Perhaps this ease came from a greater technical understanding due to my work experience and maturity in acquiring new knowledge.

A dissertation is much different from class work. The effort required is undefined, unpredictable, and usually underestimated. It always takes more time to complete a dissertation than one imagines. While I had periods during which I put my dissertation work aside to focus on SciMetrika, there were times when it felt like running a business while completing a doctoral degree added up to *more* than two jobs.

The competing demands of a growing business kept forcing the ultimate question, "Is a doctoral degree really worth it?"

By 2005, it had become clear that I did not need a doctoral degree to achieve my professional goal of being a business leader in public health rather than a researcher bent on spewing out an endless series of scientific papers. Due to my need to grow a business and take proper care of both my employees and my clients, I decidedly wanted to fry more fish than obtain another degree.

Somehow, I summoned my resolve and overcame the fact that fulfilling all the requirements of having a doctoral degree by the spring semester of 2007 was no longer necessary.

Thus, at 37, I had achieved what could be called "the ultimate success of the ego," a condition in which you have conquered your greatest fear as a child. For me, this was the fear of being unable to provide for myself or my kids; that is, not having control over what I deemed sufficient to live. I had always seen education as being the ultimate piece to achieving that control. Besides being a business owner, the doctorate in biostatistics gave me more security.

Through the lens of the child who felt that he could not even trust his parents, success meant my achieving a state in which I would always have control over my life circumstances. It meant continuously reaching beyond one's prior attainments, climbing to the highest rung of the academic ladder with a career status that guaranteed that I no longer had to worry about earning a living. With these in place, I was sure my fulfillment would be complete.

This is when I started having questions—with "What's next?" foremost among them. I had set goals for where I wanted to be by the time I reached 40, but not beyond that. Other similar questions were: "What meaning do I want my life to have? When I am on my deathbed, what would matter most to me? Would it be the stuff I've acquired? Would it be the degrees or building a business empire?"

Let's just say that what rang loudest and clearest was the certainty that neither multiple academic degrees nor an impressively extensive business empire would provide the sense of inner fulfillment I was seeking. But then, immediately in its wake, came the second question: "What *would*?"

Immediately, the thing that came to me was the satisfaction that I could touch many people through my work, including those outside of my family. There is a great sense of satisfaction from seeing young employees go from living in an apartment to buying their first house or seeing them grow into managers (and some into leaders) in a company you founded. Yes, knowing that I could touch and inspire others (some even indirectly) would give me the sense that my journey on Earth had contributed to something worthwhile.

However, I sensed that this would not be enough. It took me a few years to find the answer—or at least a path to it.

The childhood persona of a Lone Wolf that I had developed pushed me to seek power over my external circumstances. With that persona came a need to control things to feel safe. For others, it may not be power; it could be possessions or relationships.

One of the key lessons that I discovered in my quest of what would satisfy me or what I should pursue with my life is that, in the first place, my life was not about me; I was about life (*I learned this particular lesson from *Immortal Diamond: The Search for Our True Self* by Richard Rohr). This meant that I did not have to seek to control anything; instead, I only needed to be present to life. At any given time, I had the most important treasure, Source or G-d within me.

In other words, I found out that while I was seeking to pursue materiality (turning water into butter) or the certainty that I would not go hungry, I already had everything I needed within me. The message was, "If you have a treasure like a magical water that satisfies all desires, why would you waste time pursuing something that doesn't satisfy you?"

But that was far from the only invaluable lesson I learned on my quest. Some others were that:

- This journey on Earth was just a medium for achieving that growth. The first part of that growth was rejecting that on an existential level, having power, possessions, or relationships was essential to my core.

- Having shed the mask, the next step for me in growing was to explore my inner self through tools such as meditation or introspection (I have found that long walks, moments of silence, listening to music with binaural beats and water fasting create the conditions for this inner exploration).

- Life offers us opportunities for growth through challenges, invitations for new experiences, and relationships. The latter is essential because it helps us in uniquely defining what "love" is for us; that is, in answering the questions, "Is this how I want to love?" or "Is this how I want to grow in my love?"

In sum, this is answering two interconnected questions: "How do I want to grow?" and "How do I want to love?" Part of that second question of how I want to love includes, "How do I want to contribute to others?"

The process that led me to the clarity above included attending several development workshops, including the basic and advanced Landmark® Forums (http://www.landmarkforum.com) and seminars specifically for executives. Regarding the latter, I will forever be grateful to a firm called Dorrier Underwood (http://www.dorrierunderwood.com) for leading these workshops and coaching for several years. While their materials follow similar philosophies and constructs to the Landmark®, I'm glad I chose to do both. While their respective conceptual frameworks might be the same, I got a deeper understanding of the different trainings involved in service of that common goal.

One of the messages I received from both Dorrier Underwood and the Landmark Forum is that, as humans, we create stories. Events happen in our lives, and we add interpretations or meanings to them. What we consider "real" is questionable; these stories are not real. A common message from both organizations is that "humans are meaning-making machines."

One of the stories we carry with us is the first instance when we remember the experience of separation, which can be in the form of "I don't belong," "something is off," or "I am not worthy." From this event, we develop a persona and a coping mechanism. We tell ourselves stories. We let those stories drive us. This affects how we interact with others including how we listen to them.

Both organizations gave me an awareness of how I was operating and showing up in the world. For the first time, I realized I could change the stories I told myself because I could interpret them differently.

One of the realizations for me was that the story I'd told myself about being a Lone Wolf had turned me into an egotistical person solely focused on himself. I had tunnel vision where the world was all about me, and in the process, I wasn't even aware that I was causing a lot of collateral damage in pursuing my dreams.

Another component that led me to the answers I sought was the writings of a Franciscan priest named Father Richard Rohr. A few of his books that were instrumental to me include *Immortal Diamond: The Search for Our True Self* and *Falling Upward.* (1, 2)

Father Richard Rohr gave me another sense of my identity in my relationship with the Creator. He exposed me to the first definition of the "True Self," which is that it is the part of me that "is in Source and a part of Source that is in me."(1) This definition of the True Self echoes the teachings of other mystics, such as Teilhard de Chardin, who was first cited in Chapter 4(3). I mentioned that Teilhard de Chardin captured this idea with the saying "En pasi, panta Theos" (that is, "G-d is all in all," which is taken from the Bible verse 1 Corinthians 15:28). Another restatement of this message is by the poet Sufi Rumi, who stated: "We are not a drop of water in the ocean, we are the ocean in a drop of water."

The idea inherent to the True Self is that we are one of the many manifestations of Source or the Universe, as is everyone else. I found this identity more empowering than a Lone Wolf's. The way I saw it (and continue to see it) is that the latter—the Lone Wolf—is what shows up by default if I'm not conscious. However, this inner part of me has the imago Dei, which is always available for me to tap into.

Here are the questions that this definition raised for me:

- "So, how do I live the best version of myself, which combines these two?"
- "Given that my Lone Wolf character is always lurking, how do I live a life where I consciously tap into the True Self when appropriate?"
- "How do I live more consciously?"

I am still seeking answers to the above questions. One way I am currently leaning is that it has to do with how we choose to express love.

The most crucial impact of Father Rohr's teaching is that it shattered my concept of religion and spirituality. Being born into an evangelical upbringing, dogmas for attaining salvation, such as being baptized and being obedient to G-d were non-negotiable. Father Rohr introduced a new word into my vocabulary: "orthopraxy," instead of "orthodoxy."

Orthopraxy is the *right* practice (from the Greek, the root *ortho* is right like orthogonal angles), and orthodoxy is the *right* doctrine. St Francis didn't engage in squabbling regarding doctrines with leaders of the Church. He chose to practice Love.

So, how do we practice love?

I have come to accept that love—like most things from the Universe—has this dual aspect, which is, on one part, to love others as we love ourselves and, on the other, to love others as they wish to be loved. The first is called the "Golden Rule," while the other is called the "Platinum Rule."

These two rules may sometimes conflict. How we want to be treated may differ from someone else's expectations. For example, do we keep giving someone a fish instead of teaching them to fish, even though they prefer the latter? What if continuously giving them that fish stunts their ability to grow?

<hr />

In January 2010 (just before I turned 40), a massive "once in a generation" earthquake in Haiti claimed hundreds of thousands of lives and displaced a large part of the population in Port-au-Prince, during which time many were forced to live in tent enclaves.

This event had a profound impact on me. The lifeless bodies I saw on television, deprived of their humanity, naked, covered in sand, and lying in the streets reminded me of the undeserved blessings I had been the beneficiary of. Like many Haitians who have emigrated, I had planned to help when my kids were older or when I had retired. With the earthquake, however, I felt there was an urgency for me to be part of the solution—now and not later. To quote Barack Obama, "There was the urgency of *now*!"

It can be said that 2010 represents a significant milestone in my life, not merely because I turned 40 that year. The shift happened with the earthquake. The first part of my life before that event had been focused on me, on achieving my personal goals and getting as much as I could from life. After 2010, instead of pursuing individual goals, I shifted toward helping as many people as possible—particularly those in Haiti.

Before 2010, one reason I wasn't as involved in Haiti was the insecurity and political instability there. But after the crisis, this became less of a concern. My reasoning was simple: if the 10 million people in Haiti could face these dangers day in and day out, I could also endure such situations. My life was not more valuable than theirs.

So, a month after the earthquake, I visited Haiti to check on some of the extended family members who were still there and assess how I could best help. This was only my second return visit after my initial departure in 1980. My first trip had been only a few years earlier to attend the funeral of my father-in-law at the time.

The devastation was still visible upon leaving the airport, as if the earthquake had happened less than a week ago. Even at the first roundabout after exiting the airport, I saw the first of many "tent" cities sprawled around the capital. On the drive to my hotel, we passed streets that were still dense with debris, reducing already narrow streets to a maze that needed to be spatially negotiated with the drivers of the oncoming traffic.

In the debris of the many houses that were destroyed, there were many roofs that remained intact on top of their respective floors or foundations. I have heard some people refer to it as a "pancake effect," which is said to be evidence of poor construction quality. There wasn't much left to the imagination as to what could have happened to anyone caught inside the house at the time.

You would think that the shock of such an event, the loss of life of loved ones, and the precarious living conditions would have created a traumatized population and that the despair would be palpable. But even among people living in houses that were partially destroyed or makeshift tents that were unlikely to shelter them from heavy rain (let alone a tropical storm), I saw something else—something entirely unexpected.

I saw people actively going about their business and living life.

For example, when I visited my cousins in my hometown of Croix-des-Bouquets, one of them (Achilles) still lived in my maternal grandmother's house. This made it easy for me to find the house, as it was near a well-known landmark—a former presidential compound built by Baby Doc Duvalier.

When I arrived in the courtyard, several men were gathered around a game of dominoes, while in the background, the radio was broadcasting a game of soccer. In typical Haitian fashion, some were commenting on the soccer game, while others were watching the four at the table, offering commentary once the outcome of a game had been decided.

Interspaced with the loud noises of dominoes, there would be lively comments regarding the soccer scenario:

"If my team continues dominating like that on offense, a goal is surely coming soon."

Or one of the attentive observers of the domino game might offer something like:

"Wow, you gave the game away. Why not play a four-dot to support your partner instead of the two-dotted dominoes?"

The typical raw sense of humor and *joie de vivre* had not been irretrievably buried beneath the rubble.

Another example came from our driver, Philippe, a childhood friend of my former brother-in-law, Junior. We were going up a hill, and like most roads in Haiti, the roadway had no guard rails. Thus, with any slip or miscalculation, we could end up in a ditch with the worst imaginable outcome. Philippe made an abrupt maneuver, and Junior remarked in a matter-of-fact voice (but also jokingly):

"Philippe, I don't think you realize that the American doctor who treated you is gone. If an accident happens now, don't expect to get out of it like you did during the earthquake."

Philippe had been in a house from which he'd managed to escape, although not before sustaining some injuries that caused him to be hospitalized.

During the trip around Port-au-Prince and my hometown with Junior and Philippe, they brought me back up to speed on the music groups and artists in vogue. To my delight and Junior's chagrin, a vibrant style of Haitian rap music had taken root there in my absence. If there were a Grammy for international rap music, I did not doubt that some of the artists I had listened to would be very competitive prospects—including Fantom, Izolan, and Princess Eud.

Sadly, one of the groups we listened to was Barikad Crew, which they described as "the best Rap Kreyol group, hands down." They had lost their youngest member to the earthquake, as well as several more to a prior road accident. The lyrics of one of their songs, "Enjoy Your Life" (*Jwi la vi ou*), foretell their early demise and encourage us to enjoy life, as we may know at any time how many days we have lived thus far but never just how many—or few—we have left.

I called my cousin Berda to recount what I had seen.

"You know, I can't believe how resilient people are. They are going about their business. They're listening to soccer games on the radio, playing dominoes; the streets are busy with people peddling something—you might never know that they had been through a very traumatic event."

Berda responded:

"What do you want them to do—cry? They have no choice. They *have* to go on. Life continues. They have to live!"

My time in the post-earthquake Haiti was a spiritual experience. I felt that I belonged. This belonging went beyond blood and having in common a mutual birthplace.

No—I sensed some more profound connection.

The traditional IFA religions native to Africa say that when Olarun ("the Creator") sends a soul to Earth, there is a planning session beforehand. I imagine that if this were true and that before their incarnation on Earth, there is some sort of planning and pre-knowledge involved, then it must be the case that only the bravest of souls choose a disaster-prone land like Haiti.

The fraternity I sensed there might stem from the Haitian colloquial saying, 'Hope keeps you alive' (lespwa fè viv). I found myself both in awe and deeply inspired by my Haitian brethren's resiliency and unbreakable spirit. Our contribution to the brotherhood of mankind may lie in being a living testimony to the resiliency of the human spirit.

This caused a shift in my sense of identity. Instead of seeing myself as the Lone Wolf, I realized that what had propelled me was not merely my efforts alone. Whatever I had accomplished thus far came not primarily because of my efforts but more so because I was the product fashioned centuries (perhaps even millennia) ago from spiritual giants whose motto was to never give up on hope and to trust that as long as they had any shred of consciousness ("life-breath"), they could find a way through to recovery and renewal.

The other transformation that happened is that I came into a different relationship with death. I had a renewed zest for living "my life" and not one dictated by arbitrary societal norms. My feelings are captured by the poet Julia Esquivel of Guatemala in the poem *I Am Not Afraid of Death*.

I Am Not Afraid of Death

I am no longer afraid of death,
I know well
its dark and cold corridors
leading to life
I am afraid rather of that life
which does come out of death
which cramps our hands
and retards our march
I am afraid of my fear
and even more of the fear of others,
who do not know where they are going,
who continue clinging
to what they consider to be life
which we know to be death
I live each day to kill death
I die each day to beget life
and in this dying unto death,
I die a thousand times and
am reborn another thousand
through that love
from my People,
which nourishes hope!

— Julia Esquivel
Threatened with Resurrection,
1982, Elgin Press

This new identity, characterized by the quality of living without fear, would serve me well in several unexpected events that would soon come into my life.

References for Chapter 7

1. Rohr, R. (2013). *Immortal diamond: The search for our true self*. Jossey-Bass.

2. Rohr, R. (2011). *Falling upward: A spirituality for the two halves of life*. Jossey-Bass.

3. Teilhard de Chardin, P. (1960). *The divine milieu* (B. Wall, Trans.). Harper & Row. (Original work published 1957)

CHAPTER 8

Confronting the Worst Possible Fear
(2013–2015)

*"The faith of the bird is not in the strength of the branch;
but in the power of its wings."*
— (Author Unknown)

I wrote the couple of paragraphs that follow this one in the Summer of 2015 as part of a post on my blog site, *Ayipreneur*. Little did I know then that there were already events in motion that would make this a very relevant message for me.

"Imagine a bird on a branch; clearly the concern is not in the branch and what might happen to it. It seems obvious that the faith of the bird is not in how strong the branch might be but rather in its ability to react even if something happened to the branch.

"Strangely enough for us human beings, we want to put our faith in the branch or external circumstances. There are so many things that we cannot control such as the economy, what happens in our job, people who decide to depart our life. However, we can control how we flap our 'wing'; that is how we respond to these circumstances."

◦→— —◦→

It was an October morning in 2013, like any other, when I arrived at the office. Before I had even sat down, I noticed a thick white envelope on the desk, sent via certified mail. When I opened it, my jaw dropped.

It was a letter from the US Department of Justice informing me of a Civil Investigative Demand (CID). It informed me that several allegations had been made against SciMetrika, including one claiming that we had made misrepresentations to US government agencies and used unfair competitive practices to win contracts—and even more damaging, it was questioning our billing practices (specifically, how we charged time on projects), which essentially meant we had been accused of stealing from the government.

The government demanded that we give them at least 10 years' worth of data, including taxes, all communications with government agencies, all communications with employees, all proposals, contracts, and employee manuals. They seemed to be asking for virtually every record we had since we had gone into business.

After catching my breath, I went to my COO (Chief Operating Officer) and handed her the letter from the Department of Justice. She looked at it and said, "Shit... this is bad."

So then, how did this happen?

One of my former Vice Presidents (Clyde)* walked into my office one day and told me I had to choose between him and our Human Resources Director.

"It's Lisa or me," he began. "She doesn't know what she's doing and is creating more work for me." This was an ultimatum. He thought he was too big to be fired and believed that if I *did* fire him, other critical senior staff would leave with him, and we would crumble. What I heard was, "You must surrender. You have no choice."

The decision for me was easy. When he left my office, I called our IT Department and asked them to remove his access. I then walked to his office to inform him that I had decided to end his employment.

Following his termination, he threatened to sue us and asked for a ridiculous payout of $500,000 or equity. He informed us

---

* Name changed for privacy.

through his lawyer that he would destroy the company by accusing us of malpractice if we didn't settle with him. I jokingly told my lawyer: "If he thinks we are so bad, he should just go to the Justice Department. Does he need the address?"

And that is precisely what he *did*.

Under the Obama administration, there was an emphasis on fraud, waste, and abuse. The DOJ had been given additional resources to identify healthcare fraud. You would think this was only for investigating matters such as providers selling unneeded medical equipment to seniors or doctors or charging for services not provided. However, it turns out that this also covered contractors like us who had business with the Department of Health and Human Services (DHHS).

If a company were found to have obtained funds from the government on pretenses or through fraud, they would have to pay three times the amount they had received.

Clyde had engaged two other disgruntled SciMetrika employees to file what's called a "Qi Tam case." This refers to a party suing on behalf of the federal government. The Justice Department can choose whether or not to join the case. Those who file the lawsuits are called "relators." If the government wins the lawsuit, the relators receive one-third of the funds recovered.

While this was a civil investigation, it was clear that it would quickly become a criminal matter if they found any pattern or proof of willful wrongdoing. A CEO from one of my peer groups warned me: "The government will threaten death so that, by contrast, disease will be seen as acceptable." By "death," he meant a lengthy prison sentence and the seizure of all monies and assets.

And so, rather than indulging in the luxury of panic or resentment, I realized that appropriate actions needed to be taken immediately. There was a deadline by which to make these documents available. I immediately reached out to our law firm and got their resident expert on these matters, Tony, who had previously worked for the DOJ dealing with these issues from the opposite side as a prosecutor.

My attitude from the get-go was to cooperate with the government fully, give them everything they asked for, and promptly disclose any errors if it was found that we had made any.

The lawyers suggested that they conduct fact-finding so that if anything was improper, they would uncover it and report it to the DOJ. This involved interviewing any employee referenced in the case or in a senior position.

Because these employees were placed in a situation where they had legal exposure, we had to hire independent lawyers who were not affiliated with our corporate lawyers. All this caused our legal meter expenses to run high. However, the highest-ticket expense was the cost engendered in producing innumerable requested documents on a server, which allowed them to be searched interactively by the DOJ.

Aside from the costs directly related to the case, we also made operational changes that had an impact. For starters, we revamped our code of ethics, provided training on government rules, and stressed that compliance was a key component of our *modus operandi*. For a consulting firm, having vendors offer training constitutes only a tiny part of the overall expenses. The most significant negative financial factor is having employees who can engage in income-generating activities such as client work take non-billable training classes.

And yet, no cost was greater than the dramatic reduction in our growth momentum. Until the appearance of this lawsuit, we had been in an extended period of exponential growth. As I mentioned in the previous chapter, we had such a high growth rate that we made the Inc Magazine list of fastest-growing companies twice in 2011 and 2012. With this lawsuit, however, we had no option but to slow down.

The reason for this loss in momentum was that many of the contracts we were pursuing required a company to disclose if there was an active investigation. Our lawyers had advised us that we had every reason to keep the investigation quiet. Knowing that we were under investigation could easily spook a government agency, and it might take us out of the running for the contract anyway.

The real possibility was that this could have spelled the end of SciMetrika and my life as I knew it. There was even the threat of my being imprisoned, losing all I had earned and achieved, and having to start my life all over again.

My friends told me I should expect the DOJ to find something. "Remember, they have to justify their salary. They have to find something to justify their effort. Even if you are not guilty, they might find a minor violation and then make a big deal out of it." One of my employees, David, told me about a former contractor who had been threatened with jail for errors that totaled less than $25,000 in excessive billings.

Some of my friends who knew me well were worried because they knew I was more of a "big picture" type of leader and tended not to focus on the details. I often heard, "Everyone makes mistakes; if they look hard enough, they are bound to find some error that they could say was willful wrongdoing." One of the analogies I frequently heard was that this invasive scrutiny on the part of the bureaucracy was like a colonoscopy… but without the benefit of any anesthesia.

My friends didn't appreciate that I was very aware that I tended not to pay attention to the details—and because of that, I made sure I had someone who *did*. Jessica, my polar opposite regarding the minutiae, was in charge of our contracts; additionally, she was the most ethical person I knew and remained so to this day.

Throughout the investigation, I successfully remained at peace. I slept well and did not waste time crying or cursing my fate; I simply lived my life.

My calm demeanor troubled some of my employees. Jessica asked for a meeting and told me:

"You are not taking this investigation seriously. I haven't been able to sleep. My career will be *ruined* if SciMetrika is found to have violated the rules."

My response was:

"Jessica, what do you want me to do—*cry*? How will that solve anything? I have confidence I have done nothing wrong. All I can do is do my best and let the Universe take care of the rest."

Jessica wasn't the only employee who was rattled by the investigations. My COO then asked me several times, "What is your gut telling you? Do you think you'll make it through this?"

I'm guessing she didn't believe we would make it. At one point, she told me I should have initiated a conversation to increase her compensation. She even suggested I turn control over to her so that my family could be provided for in case I went to prison.

Facing this chaos, here is the mental attitude I adopted:

- **Attitude 1: "This is a first-world problem."** That is to say; this is the type of problem for people who are blessed to live in a country like the US, as opposed to a third-world country. When friends and others asked me how I was coping, I told them this was precisely how I saw it. There was no way I could call a family member or a friend in Haiti and share what I was dealing with.

I could hear between my friends' many comments and concerns, "But you could go to jail!" However, that risk is simply part of the job in the industry I had chosen to work in. I was in the "government services" industry, which is heavily regulated. The risk of an audit or investigation is higher than that of other industries. While it was true that I could have gone to jail, it is equally true that I was blessed to be able to afford the best legal defensive team.

- **Attitude 2: "How could I turn this "bitter water into butter?"**—which is to say, how could I transform this daunting challenge into a winning proposition? More specifically, I would ask the question: "Years from now, if I were to tell the story of this situation from the perspective that it had ultimately been a blessing in disguise, *in what specific way (or ways)* would it have been a blessing? Exactly *how* would I have been able to leverage it?"

I was in a CEO peer group called Vistage, and this is a question that I pondered with my group and discussed with my executive team at SciMetrika. One of our commitments was to come out of this situation with a strong culture of compliance. We had vowed that when others looked at us, they would see us as a "company known to have the highest ethical standards."

- **Attitude 3: "This situation is like spilled milk."** This was a perspective offered to me by a CEO friend, Greg, who was in my Vistage group and ran a holding company.

"Think of it this way: if you spill milk and are crying afterward, you should ask yourself, 'Why am I not crying after an expensive bottle of wine?' And if you are crying after an expensive bottle of wine, you should ask yourself, 'Why am I not in a position where I have so much expensive wine that I'll need more than one lifetime to finish drinking my collection?'" He continued: "In your case, this would be spilled milk if you had a holding company and SciMetrika was a small part of a large portfolio."

- **Attitude 4: "I shall be an example of how one can go through this with grace and a winning attitude."** I kept asking myself, "What is the best way to deal with this problem?" That's all I wanted to know, and then I could let the Universe take care of the rest. No crying. No whining. Be at my best and let what I can't control unfold.

My advice for anyone going through a similar agonizing event is that the most important thing is who you are in the moment rather than what you do. In other words, how are you showing up?

To be crystal clear, while I knew I would make it through this crisis, I did not know exactly what "making it" would look like. Would it be that they would find some inadvertent errors, and the company would have to pay a fine? Would the investigation make us bleed so much money that our bank might call our loans? While I was sure that we would prevail—which, for me, only meant that they would not find any willful wrongdoing (and, therefore, no jail time), I knew that even this could lead to financial catastrophe.

Here is a quote that I used throughout this process and similar crises:

"You must never confuse faith that you will prevail in the end—which you can never afford to lose—with the discipline to confront the most brutal facts of your current reality, whatever they might be."

This quote is by Admiral Stockdale and comes from the book *Good to Great* by Jim Collins (1). I value it because of its emphasis on balancing the need to recognize the seriousness of a given situation with the necessity for maintaining optimism, even in the face of that seriousness.

Admiral Stockdale had been a prisoner during the Vietnam War. He observed that those prisoners who didn't make it psychologically were the ones who would tell themselves, "We are going to be home for Christmas," or "We will be free in a few months," because a time constraint would set possibly unrealistic parameters on that faith.

In hindsight, when I look at how I've gone through crises, my strong suit has been optimism. In contrast, my weakness has been my tendency to underestimate just how bad things can become, as well as failing to maintain an awareness of the need for contingency plans to address various possible outcomes.

The one scenario I failed to allow for was that even though we might survive the investigation (which we did), the ordeal might still result in permanently stunting our growth in such a way that instead of sudden death, surviving this investigation could lead to a slow death.

It took us more than a year—until February of 2015—to find out that the DOJ had closed the file on us. They didn't ask for an interview with us or a meeting with our lawyers. After not hearing from them for a long time, I asked our attorney to inquire about the status. That's when they sent us the letter telling us they had ended their investigation and the disgruntled employees had dropped their case.

We had won... and, most critically, *I* had won.

But I had failed to realize just what a toll the battle had taken. It wasn't the money we had spent (more than a million dollars), the impact on employee morale, or the loss of our touch for writing winning proposals. While I have no proof of this, I suspect that the investigation—which had to involve the DOJ asking questions of our clients—might have spooked them or given them a reason to draw back from doing business with us.

This is one of the sad consequences of all accusations: whether justified or unjustified, once they are made, the risk of potential guilt they carry tends to remain embedded (consciously or unconsciously) in the minds of past or future clients.

While I didn't envision losing market share and seeing revenue decrease after the investigation, I knew we had to diversify. That part of our growth in the future would have to come from venues outside of those provided by the government. To that end, we started looking for future acquisitions.

In November 2015, we found a suitable opportunity around which to create the current company I oversee, called ScitoVation. Had I been disciplined and envisioned all possible outcomes, the next step after emerging from the investigation would have been to sell SciMetrika as soon as possible.

I sold SciMetrika in 2018 for a price three to five times lower than what it would have sold for in 2015—less than 2 million dollars, whereas in 2018, it could have quickly sold for between 7 and 10 million.

I share this not because I have regrets about what I might have done differently but because of my conviction as to the necessity of sustaining the tension of the two poles of the Stockdale Paradox—i.e., that of maintaining the faith that we would ultimately prevail while at the same confronting the hard facts of how things might still go awry.

And so, I came to see in time that the crucible of the investigation by the DOJ had been a blessing in disguise—and that it would ultimately set in motion events that would wind up transforming my identity as I knew it.

The experience of going through the DOJ episode forced me to face what I had considered the worst possible fear: being in a situation of not having control of the outcome (and, in this case, not even the process). If the DOJ lawyers had found evidence of fraud and gone for a criminal investigation with unlimited resources, this would have been a fatal blow to my Ego.

The expenses and time that would be required for criminal defense if that had been their determination would have depleted any savings while at the same time crippling my ability to earn an income. Forget about the possibility of incarceration—how would I have taken care of my family in preparation for (and during) a trial?

By default, in any given situation, having no control over the process is as frightening to me as the outcome. While I was very confident that I had done nothing wrong, there was still the possibility that there could be some errors in billing or actions by others in a company of more than 150 people, which might have escaped our oversight. What I felt was like some kind of tiny parasite eating one's flesh away so slowly that you didn't feel the pain. Still, you knew that eventually, you would experience pain, a pain that would increase in intensity until a harrowing death.

It is very difficult for people of my personality type to sit and wait. I often have a bias toward action. In the mindset of someone who likes to control their environment, taking action provides the comforting sense that you can affect the outcome. This is one instance where there was nothing else I could do even if I had wanted to—beyond cooperating fully with the government and taking steps to be even more rigorous (outlined earlier).

This situation required me to surrender and accept that in this life, we cannot control everything. As part of life, we should also trust that after we have done everything we need to do, whatever outcome presents itself is the best one. It works for us and the greater good, even if it doesn't appear so in the moment.

Surrendering means not being attached to the outcome. In the case of a grave illness, for example, this would mean accepting that it may progress to death. For me, it meant the possibility that some errors might have been uncovered from the investigation, with consequences ranging from civil penalties (which could spell the end of the company) to criminal charges (which could lead to prison).

Once I had accepted that my life was not about me and that I was about life, I had entered into far deeper spiritual waters. This was arguably the greatest lesson for the control freak who considered himself "The Lone Wolf" and felt compelled to be in charge in every instance..

However, life wasn't yet finished with me. A lesson about love—the fuel of the Universe, the Essence of Creation, the Divine Logos—awaited me. It is the subject of the next chapter.

Reference for Chapter 8

1. Collins, J. (2001). *Good to great: Why some companies make the leap... and others don't*. HarperCollins.

CHAPTER 9

Our Essence is Infinite Love

"The opposite of love is not hate, it's indifference."

— Elie Wiesel

When the Department of Justice investigation ended in 2015, I had been married for 21 years. But that investigation had not made a dent in our marriage. In fact, in 2015 and 2016, our relationship was as strong as ever.

I never shared the full extent of the DOJ investigations with my family, including the potential criminal liabilities that could have been levied upon me. What I chose to communicate to Valery, my wife at the time, was the assurance that we would ultimately prevail. There was no discussion of what might have happened had the case had an adverse outcome.

I communicated even less about the situation to my kids. It is 2024 as I write this, and it was only a couple of months ago that I shared the lawsuit document from the DOJ with either Valery or our children.

Even while we were married, I lived a compartmentalized life. I avoided bringing anything up to Valery that might upset her. One area in which I kept things to myself was regarding work issues. If they were critical—whether it was a lawsuit, the loss of a major client, a deficit in the business, or layoffs—I might mention it in passing but not share any details.

Why didn't I share more, one might ask? Part of the reason was that I believed it was my responsibility to solve the problem. The other is that I felt that Valery was more emotional than I was and, therefore, more likely to inhabit a state of fear if she were aware of the details—with no doubt equally destructive effects upon our children. I wanted more than anything to avoid the emotions that would almost inevitably come upon her having to contemplate the worst-case scenarios, which would require me (in some measure) to activate my fears along with her.

In dealing with any situation—especially problematic ones—my lifelong choice was always to take action, as I believed that, more often than not, negative emotions like fear or anxiety were more of a nuisance than a help. My attitude was simply to marginalize them in the moment and not let them get in the way of intelligent action.

I assumed that having a spouse who embodied the wisdom of, "I got this!" or "It's already been taken care of," and whose prevailing attitude was, "You worry about the home front—the kids and family affairs—and I'll handle everything else," was what she needed and wanted.

In retrospect, another area in which I kept things compartmentalized and shared far too little—in typical male fashion—was concerning what was going on inside me, including not only how I was feeling but also how I was evolving spiritually and personally, as well as in my ever-evolving philosophy of life; even though I would certainly share various books that I had read or new concepts I had come across with her. But I have now seen that these were, at best, poor substitutes for the direct, honest emotional exchange that so many women need from their partners.

And in what I had assumed was sparing her anything that I deemed might rock the boat, I had unknowingly planted the seeds for what would become a final alienation between us.

When we met, we were both evangelical Christians who believed in the literal interpretation of the Bible. One of the tenets of our faith was that God had created us to procreate ("populate the earth") and pass on our values to our children—namely, "the fear of the Lord."

Saint Exupery, the author of *The Little Prince,* defined love as two people who are not just looking at each other but also looking in the same direction. He says, "Love does not consist in gazing at each other, but in looking outward together in the same direction."

From that definition, there was undoubtedly strong love between us. In addition to our faith and the mutually felt obligation of "building for Heaven," the bond of our relationship was rooted in the fact that when we first met, we were two young Haitian immigrants who had set out to live the American dream and climb the social ladder, an ambition that was like building castles in the sky for our parents. Chief amongst them was acquiring an education and becoming card-carrying members of the American middle class with a comfortable dwelling in the suburbs.

But this wasn't a marriage created only to combine our forces to climb that social ladder. We also shared a powerful romantic love; Valery is gorgeous, and we had a dynamic mutual attraction. While I would not point to physical attraction as my strongest suit, there was still no question that we were both madly in love.

In fact, after our divorce, I realized that she loved me more than she had ever dared let me know, perhaps out of fear of being seen as needy or possibly being loved less thereby.

But I discovered that the truth of the matter is no amount of physical attraction can maintain a healthy relationship over the long term if there is no spiritual connection. The breaking down of our marriage was eloquent proof of that.

And as to the breakdown of our faith, based on several of my friends' quizzical looks, I imagine they were asking, "How could someone who believes in science accept a literal interpretation of the Bible, including the creation in seven days?"

I've long had doubts about this notion, even as a child. My insight about the relevance of scientific verification in Biblical narratives has been that even if God had explained creation to the most intelligent man at the time, it would have been doomed to failure.

113

Even now, it would be incredibly difficult for a modern PhD scientist (let alone for the humans of antiquity) to genuinely understand the mysteries of the creation of the Universe.

No—*my problem with the Bible wasn't its inconsistency with known scientific facts but its inconsistency with love.*

In any faith, there is always some healthy dose of skepticism; it is encouraged. To quote Voltaire: "Faith consists in believing when it is beyond the power of reason to believe. But to have faith without reason is surrendering the mind to ignorance."

Within any faith's parameters, some principles or teachings remain that cannot be verified through pure reasoning.

If we're given a book and told that it contains the truth, there are two ways in which it can be judged: first, we can assess whether that book is consistent with itself (internal consistency), and second, we can check whether the statements in that book are consistent with other well-established parallel truths, such as historical facts (external consistency).

While I could explain the scientific inconsistencies regarding love, there came a point at which blind faith was woefully insufficient in explaining how a loving Creator could ever be compatible with the deity described in the Old Testament. I couldn't explain how a Creator who had said that "He does not visit the sins of the father upon the children" could destroy an entire nation, such as the Amalekites—a genocide (let us call it for what it was) found in the first book of Samuel (my very namesake, no less!) as a result of actions committed by a prior generation (1 Samuel 15).

Then there is the issue of slavery. I could not accept that a God so frequently described as a loving father—a Being whose essence and nature is purported to be the epitome of love—would ever treat His children as alien stepchildren and be willing to declare openly, "I love this one," (Jacob) and "I hate that one." (Esau).

It is much the same case for homosexuality. Growing up in an evangelical environment, I had accepted early on from the teachings

114

of the Gospel that homosexuality was more than simply abnormal; that it was evil and an abomination. When I joined the workplace, however, I met various colleagues who were in the LGBTQ (Lesbian, Gay, Bisexual, Transgender, and Queer) community who, counterintuitively, turned out to be the most caring people of all. How could I square that with the teachings of a God who, at one point, commanded that they should be stoned to death?

Starting in 2016, I was finding excuses to skip church—and when I did attend, I was present in body only and not in spirit. During the sermons, I often read a book, as I was only there to be with my family and kids.

Eventually, it became untenable for me to go to church at all. Attending felt palpably insincere. By the end of 2016, I stopped going.

The changes in my spiritual life went beyond my lack of church attendance. The ritual in our family was to pray together every night. As part of that ritual, we would also read from a quarterly workbook that contained the spiritual teachings of the Adventist Church, which we referred to as "Sabbath school lessons," but these lessons felt inauthentic, as did the prayers.

I no longer believed in an anthropomorphic God seated upon a high throne and demanding to be worshiped, ready at any and every given moment to strike us down, Zeus-like, with a lightning bolt or trident for any minor offense. My view of the Creator had changed from one who is external (and therefore separate) to one who is an inseverable part of me and of whom I, in turn, am an inseverable part.

I came to believe that the Creator, in His or Her—or Its—Omnipresence, permeates every organ, tissue, cell, molecule, atom, and sub-atomic particle of my being and that there is nowhere I can ever go or exist without being imbued with the presence of Him/Her/It; that wherever I happen to find myself, my Maker, my Source, is (and will always be) with—and within—me.

However, my spiritual evolution was only part of my marital issues.

One of the tensions in the marriage was that pursuing my graduate studies—a master's degree and then a doctorate—had created resentment in our relationship. Valery felt that she was giving more to the marriage than I was. As a result of taking care of the kids and maintaining the household, she could not pursue her educational aspirations. On my end, I felt that I had sacrificed a lot as well and I was being unappreciated.

Valery and I separated at the beginning of 2020, just before the advent of the COVID era. While I could say there were probably many factors that led to the end of our marriage, once I had made the conscious decision not to go through the motions and follow routines such as going to church, it became even more apparent that we no longer belonged together. We were merely roommates staying under the same roof only because of religious traditions that said it had to be so under an order from God. I never bought into the idea that a couple should stay married for the sake of their children. That reason didn't exist for us, either. All our kids were adults by then. Our only child, who had not graduated from college, lived in a group home.

Beginning in late 2018, we lived separately under the same roof. Even though we did not share the same marital bed, this did not reduce tensions between us. If anything, it made things worse.

Some things were said that don't deserve to be repeated. Words were impulsively uttered that had the emotional impact of being repeatedly stabbed with an invisible knife, as if one were emotionally bleeding out from the deep, maliciously inflicted wounds—then somehow being resurrected, only to be stabbed yet again. Suffice it to say that in all my years (even those spent living in the embattled territory of the southern US), I've never felt more humiliated and denigrated than I did in the period following my separation.

Yet, I don't consider myself a victim. In any long-term relationship, the difference between perpetrators and victims is thin. I do know that whatever was said to me did not come from a place of love but out of someone who was in a state of extreme pain—and felt that I was responsible for causing it.

I underestimated the degree to which Valery felt humiliated by the end of the marriage. I failed to recognize the extent to which her core identity was that of a mother and wife. She saw the end of the marriage as a rejection and an abandonment.

The complete breakdown in our relationship occurred in September of 2020. This was when I informed Valery that I had met the love of my life, Jala, and that I felt this relationship harbored the potential to go the distance. For me, it was a matter of fairness and at the same time, living in authenticity. I had erroneously assumed that she had moved on, but Valery saw it as a betrayal because our divorce had not yet been finalized.

Jala and I met in July 2020. When we did, I wasn't looking for a relationship. At this point in my life, I thought I would be a bachelor for the remainder of the earthly journey. On the meditation app "Insight Timer," I noticed that Jala appeared to be meditating while I was. Usually, I meditate early in the morning (5:30–6:00 a.m.). Even on those days when I altered my schedule, we would both be on the app. It also turned out that we had many teachers in common.

Our relationship started with the following message on the app: "I've noticed that we have similar interests in meditating; I'd like to get to know you if you are open to it."

It turned out that I had used the magic word ("open"), as this was her chosen word for the year.

Before a Zoom meeting scheduled for July, I suggested we share our enneagram personality assessment. I have used this assessment for key relationships, including business.

The Enneagram is not about right or wrong. It's an assessment that categorizes personalities into nine types, where the name "enneagram" comes from. The underlying theory behind the enneagram is that at some point early in life, we experience rejection, lack of love, or some other sense of something being amiss with our world and to adapt, we develop a persona or personal role through which to deal with the challenge.

As part of that persona, we have default tendencies in approaching life. The enneagram also describes the behaviors we resort to when stressed. My personality is what's called a "Type 8," and one of the fears of Type 8 people is that of being controlled. When we met via Zoom and discussed our personality assessments, we talked about our stories thus far. We took turns discussing the moments we felt we did not belong and the personas we developed from our loss of innocence.

Happily, our first meeting was a hit. Less than two weeks later, in the middle of the COVID-19 frenzy, we decided to meet face-to-face halfway between Durham, North Carolina, and Pittsburgh, Pennsylvania.

As I was looking on the Airbnb website, zooming in and out on the map, the place I had selected somehow turned out to be much closer to me than it was to Jala—three hours from Durham and about five hours from Pittsburgh. Being a gentleman, I was looking for a place closer to Jala than me.

The place I found (called "HeartStone") was in Buena Vista, near Lexington, Virginia, on a 260-acre property that used to be a farm but was now a lodge with several cabins. The property's main attraction is a labyrinth on a hillside called "Mount Grace," with a view of four different mountain ranges, including the Appalachians. Mount Grace is also home to entities or geometric symbols that revealed themselves to Antonia (the co-owner), along with one of the family members, with whom I feel a deep connection and the presence of Infinite Love.

When I met Jala, there was no debate about how serious our relationship would be or whether we would continue to date other people. We both knew in the moment that the relationship was a gift from the Universe. This was an intuitive understanding, as opposed to a decision where one must exercise the analytical mind to determine which options to pursue and which to discard.

Jala and I have been together since July 2020. During this time, I have experienced both the extremities of the absence of love—in being rejected as humanly, spiritually "less than"—and in the liberating experience of Divine Love. I can attest to the truth of the quote by Dumbledore, the Master Wizard character from the Harry Potter universe: "Happiness can be found even in the darkest of times, if one only remembers to turn on the light."

From my first stay at HeartStone, one of the revelations I was given is that our essence is Infinite Love. When we love someone, it is a phenomenon not due to any external stimulus but rather to the fact that the "other"—whether it is human, animal, or Divine—functions as a vessel or medium similar to a mirror, reflecting the beauty of our soul to us. So, when we say, "I love you," we are saying, "You are a mirror that enables me to see the Infinite Love that is alive in me."

The second lesson is a corollary from the first one. Because our essence is Infinite (which is to say limitless) Love, we all possess the ability and capacity to love everyone. Our love can be the spark that awakens the Divine Love within someone else.

This lesson was useful for me as I was going through the painful process of divorce. There were times when I felt both pain and anger—most keenly for my prior partner. Sometimes, within the safe harbor of my mind, I could hear myself screaming out, "How dare you want to judge me?!" or "How could you be so knowingly mean and still dare to claim that you are serving a God of Love?"

I am aware that many spiritual gurus would say it's a bad thing to feel anger and that you should seek to repress these types of negative emotions. My approach with any emotion is to allow them to run their course, choosing to feel them and acknowledge that this is how I feel. I have found that the most effective "solvent" that allows a persistent or entrenched feeling to dissolve is awareness itself... to become fully conscious that this is what I am experiencing in the moment without attaching any judgment to the experience.

Going through these dark emotions of pain and anger, the lessons I learned about Love at HeartStone gave me hope for a better relationship with my ex-wife in the knowledge that our essence was Infinite Love. We both had it within us. With this realization, the following poem from Julia Esquivel—the Guatemalan poet I mentioned in an earlier chapter—came into my consciousness:

> **Why Not?**
> *If stars are reflected*
> *Even in puddles of mud,*
> *Why would they then not also be reflected*
> *In the most ill-fated of people?*
>
> — Julia Esquivel,
> Secrets of God's Reign, 2002

With this poem, the questions that kept arising for me were, "Why am I not able to see the Infinite Love, the glory of the Almighty in those who have hurt me?" and "Why am I not able to be a mirror that reflects to them the Infinite Love that is hidden in them?"

These questions continue to inspire me to grow in my love and give me hope that I have the power within me—Infinite Love—to transform my relationships. This is not about transforming anyone; it's about tapping into the power within me and letting my light shine, trusting that it can make a difference.

Having navigated the depth of negative emotions from a separation, I can say forcefully that transforming water into butter—that is, to materialize wealth out of poverty—is level 101 alchemy compared to changing negative emotions into love. In my case, it was anger and resentment. It might be shame, hate, disdain, fear, or indifference for others.

Indifference might be the one emotion that is the most pernicious and dangerous to us as humans. It comforts us in the absence of hostility toward others. This is one that I've always taken comfort in. It's been relatively easy for me to be completely detached from the scorn or hate of others and say to myself, "Why should I care?" or "I won't pay any attention to you."

This last stanza of the poem "If" by Rudyard Kipling resonates with me:

> If you can talk with crowds and keep your virtue,
>
> Or walk with Kings—nor lose the common touch,
>
> *If neither foes nor loving friends can hurt you,*
>
> *If all men count with you, but none too much;*
>
> If you can fill the unforgiving minute
>
> With sixty seconds' worth of distance run,
>
> Yours is the Earth and everything that's in it,
>
> And—which is more—you'll be a Man, my son!

While I have found it easy to insulate myself from the hateful behaviors or attitudes of others toward me, what I have learned is that indifference is not the answer. The transformation I'm seeking is to be indifferent to the "behavior," and not to the individual behind that behavior.

Perhaps the most extraordinary alchemy is not to turn water into butter or stone into bread but to turn our indifference toward other humans—and possibly other conscious beings—into love.

When we have negative emotions about others, we can feel that this is unnatural. If we had all conquered indifference, perhaps we might have conquered problems such as famine or preventable diseases, and we would work to end wars that don't affect us.

I have seen a powerful example of how indifference can be transformed into love. I met Bobby and Sherry Burnett, the co-founders of an organization called "Love a Child" (https://loveachild.com/) in Haiti. After a visit to the country, Sherry wanted to create an orphanage to take care of children. Bobby was resistant, telling his wife, "We can't take on these children if I cannot love them." He didn't hate the children; he simply didn't have the same love his wife had that led her to want to act.

Eventually, however, his indifference toward these children was transformed into love, and the organization they created outside of Port-au-Prince went on to build a school, a clinic, and an indoor market.

I also heard the story of Margaret Mead—an anthropologist who had been asked about the first sign of evolution in a culture. Her response wasn't about new weapons or tools but instead about a 14,000-year-old femur that had been broken and healed. In the wild, an animal with a broken leg would die—unable to run from danger, hunt, or access water. The fact that the leg had healed was evidence that someone had cared for this person, providing them with protection and food during their recovery. Mead argued that this was the first sign of civilization because it showed compassion and communal care.

I sense that another level of evolution for our species will come when we can reach within ourselves and reject the fallacy that we can be perfectly well when there is even a single other human suffering. Hence, rejecting this thought, we will aspire to turn water into butter and sorrow into joy—not just for ourselves but for all humankind.

References for Chapter 9

1. Saint-Exupéry, A. de. (1943). *The little prince* (R. Howard, Trans.). Harcourt, Brace & World.

2. Cuarón, A. (Director). (2004). *Harry Potter and the prisoner of Azkaban* [Film]. Warner Bros.

3. Esquivel, J. (2002). *Secrets of God's reign/Algunos secretos del reino: Poems* (K. Ogle, C. M. Corcoran, & J. M. Noone, Trans.). Epica Task Force

4. Kipling, R. (1910). *Rewards and fairies*. Macmillan.

CHAPTER 10

Live the Power Within

"Our deepest fear is not that we are inadequate.
Our deepest fear is that we are powerful beyond measure.
It is our light, not our darkness that most frightens us."

— Marianne Williamson

I spent most of this book describing how a persona—the Lone Wolf—was created from the combination of the environment I was born in and how I reacted to it. While to most people, this personality may appear to be odd, strange, or very different from how they see themselves, my thesis is that every human on this planet creates a persona for themselves. Sadly, most of us wear these masks as if they are the totality of our personhood. I hope this book's message rings loud and clear that we are more than small children who felt that they did not belong or that something was "off" and had to develop a coping strategy.

In sharing the story of my life thus far, I have no pretension that the circumstances I faced were more extraordinary than anyone else's—nor do I think I have achieved something so unique that it is worth sharing. I *am* sure that every one of us has to deal with challenges that include setbacks and heartbreaks. No mansion or station in life is secure enough to keep us safe from undesirable circumstances.

It is true that coming from Haiti (said to be one of the most economically disadvantaged countries on Earth), my mother and the many women in my family had to deal with a uniquely unfavorable environment in which they had to provide for themselves and their family (I say "women" because growing up, my father and the other men were mostly absent). Across cultures, there's often a phrase or expression about transforming life's challenges into something positive. Universally, we might say "turning lemons into lemonade," while in the US, similar ideas are conveyed through sayings like "making bread from stones" or "cooking stone soup."

In the context of Haiti, the colloquialism "turning water into butter" seems appropriate. I was inspired by those in my lineage and around me who have managed to make a living out of virtually nothing, where, in some cases, they took care of their children and even lent a hand to extended family members.

I also like the saying "turning water into butter" because it conveys the idea of being alchemists of the impossible. I believe this applies to all of us. If we are, why do we spend so much time worrying about material things as a species? I would argue that from our initial childhood wounds, we generally tend to pursue one of the "three P's" of "possessions, perception, or power." Possession is self-explanatory; perception can be being well-regarded by others around us, whether it's a small group (such as parents or our friends) or a larger group (fame); and power, in my case, doesn't mean having power over others—it's merely achieving a feeling that we are in control of our situation.

While it's true that my parents and the generations before me have overcome many odds, this book didn't intend to be a "how-to" guide on climbing the social ladder despite dire circumstances. However, I hope their story and the life I have lived thus far testify to the resiliency of the human spirit.

Instead, this book is an invitation to a higher level of alchemy, to live the Divine in a world designed to make us focus on more mundane matters. Before closing this book with this invitation, I want to share some key lessons I learned along this journey.

◄►— —◄►

Unbecoming: Shining the Light of the Present into the Past

Coming to this Earth and creating a persona or mask because we are bound to be subjected to rejection or feeling inadequate at some point in our childhood is all part of our human journey. One of the critical points I have made in this book is that if you look at any child in the world, wherever they are born (within the walls of a huge palace or a one-room shack), it is a virtual certainty that at some point he or she will experience a lack of love, a sense that something is off, or "I am different," along with the consequent fear that arises in its aftermath.

From that fear, a persona is created—although it may be less pronounced than a Lone Wolf. Sadly, most people live with and carry this persona throughout their lives. It's like giving someone a mask for a role in a play, and they don't just remain in character—they forget they are even playing a character and instead live as that character all the time (although every now and then, a glance of who they truly are might burst out).

This is why unbecoming is the first part of living the power within. By "unbecoming," this does not mean "annihilating" so much as it does "being aware of the small ego we have created." As long as we are alive, we will have this small self around us, too. There is no point in trying to get rid of it. The danger lies in living unconsciously as if this small self were our entire identity, to the detriment of the eternal spirit within.

By unbecoming (which is a process), the aim is to realize that, first and foremost, we are a powerful Spirit, dwelling temporarily in space and time in human form. Once we realize that, we aim to cultivate constant communion with that Spirit as much (and as often) as possible.

Years ago, there was a famous commercial for the American Express credit card that featured the tagline "Don't leave home without it"—which suggests that there is the possibility of doing just that. But this is emphatically *not* the case with our Essence. We can never leave the Spirit that lives within us—nor, conversely, does the Spirit ever have the option of departing from us. We may, for a period, forget this eternal part of our identity, but it is always there and available to us.

In sharing the story of my loss of innocence, I hope others will see it as an invitation to take an introspective look at their past, at that pivotal moment in their life when they went through a similar experience. It's also an invitation to share our story with those we have close relationships with (both personal and professional) and create an environment where they feel safe to do the same.

I had to revisit key moments of my life not just for this book but also through both organized and personal retreats. This is something I do regularly, several times a year. There is value in constantly looking back at those critical moments in life. Psychologists use the concept of "reframing" to describe the process of looking back at past events from a present angle and re-evaluating our interpretation of them.

Because we *do* change, we are likely to gain new insights each time we look back. The person we are at 45 will see the same events in our childhood differently than who we were at 25. It is the process of reframing that allowed me to change the conclusion made by a five-year-old child that he had to be in control because he couldn't trust his parents to feed him, instead adopting a narrative that was more powerful about being gifted with the vision to see the future that is different from my present circumstances.

To be clear, that first moment in our life where we lost our innocence is not the only one we should revisit. There is a lot to be gained in reviewing key moments where we have experienced success or failure. When going through these highs and lows, it is difficult (if not impossible) to have a full view of the situation. Going back and reframing these events with the benefit of the knowledge and wisdom of the present is akin to looking at a scene from various angles. Each one provides additional details.

Live the power within by reframing the past. Below are some recommendations.

Live the Power Within by Reframing the Past

— Reframe the instance where you lost your innocence. Considering your experiences and where you are now, how would you change that narrative?

— Have a practice of regularly revisiting and reframing critical moments of your life

— Use a tool such as the enneagram to become aware of your default responses based on the persona you created

— Share your enneagram and your story with those in your close circle

---

We Are Powerful Because Others Are

While I may give the impression of being proud of the Lone Wolf character, it should not be understood to mean I am promoting or glorifying this persona. What someone may take for pride is likely because my attitude has evolved into compassion toward this being created out of the mind of a young boy who was afraid for his survival. Living as the Lone Wolf or having it spontaneously show up has brought unnecessary pain to me and others. There have been many times during which I have "gone it alone," even in situations involving entrepreneurship and key decision-making, where I would have benefited from taking others with me on the journey.

Because of my commitment not to allow my life to happen by default or of being under the dictates of my Lone Wolf persona, I have adopted what I would call "radical inclusion." My stand now is that a part of us is hidden in everyone. An analogy I've used in the past is that we are all like the interwoven strands of a tapestry.

While we could choose to stand on our own and apart as an attractive, colorful, stain-resistant strand, we would all find ourselves so much firmer and more radiant when we were interwoven with others in the co-creation of our "masterpiece."

My new modus operandi is for any major initiative: "Who else needs to come with me on this journey?" While certain activities may need to be completed by a single individual (such as the creation of a work of art or piece of music), I believe these are the exceptions rather than the rule. I would even venture so far as to say that we are at our best when we are co-creating—even in co-creating—our own lives.

Recently, an overseas office of a US government agency asked me to advise on implementing their strategic plan. In the past, I would have jumped at the opportunity and run with it. This time, however, I reached out to a couple of consultants—one who was already a friend and the other because of his previous experience with the agency. Combined, we brought more value than either of us could have offered alone. Before the completion of our engagement, the client introduced us to another office, which contracted us for the same service.

In this context, the question is: if our life is a tapestry... with whom are we weaving it? Our societies have imposed a particular structure where those we create our life with are expected to be confined primarily to our intimate partner (spouse) and those who share our biological legacy, beginning with children or siblings and then broadening out (to a lesser extent) to extended family. Because we are blessed to live in an age where with the Internet, "the world is flat," and anyone can become a potential collaborator, my suggestion when "choosing your tribe" would be to consider the world to be our canvas;" or, in other words, "cast a wide net in selecting the pieces of strands with which—or whom—you will build your life tapestry."

Another analogy for our relationship with others is the idea that humans are symbionts; that is, we are like the system between a flower and a bee. Neither can exist (much less flourish) without the other. To strengthen one is to strengthen the other. When we build ourselves, we can help the groups we are part of to grow—whether these are our intimate partnerships, extended family relationships, or workplace and civic groups that we may be involved in. At the same time, if these groups grow, then the members will likewise grow.

Whatever we can accomplish alone can be exponentially multiplied when we function in groups. Research has shown that whether in the realm of professionals or students, those in a peer group tend to do better. This is not a new notion. Napoleon Hill, in his book *Think and Grow Rich* (1), suggested that everyone should have a sort of "kitchen cabinet" of trusted individuals that he calls a "mastermind group" to help them achieve their major goals.

A support group also benefits our well-being outside of the professional arena. Multiple studies have shown that the quantity and quality of life are linked to our social connections. One of the most well-known and longest-running longevity studies is The Harvard Study of Adult Development (2), which began in 1938. It tracked the lives of 724 men from diverse backgrounds in Boston over decades and later included their spouses and children. This study found that strong social ties were the most consistent predictor of health and happiness. Participants with robust relationships lived longer, had lower rates of heart disease, and experienced slower cognitive decline. Married individuals lived 5–17 years longer on average than their unmarried counterparts. The study emphasizes that while achievements and wealth matter to some extent, relationships play the most crucial role in well-being across a lifetime.

Steven Crane, a social engagement scholar at Stanford, has stated: "Our relationships form a lattice of support that constitutes the largest single factor in the overall well-being of most people." (3)

At a time when we are facing a loneliness epidemic in Western countries, it is worth emphasizing that "living the power within" does not mean tackling life alone. We are symbionts. The Lone Wolf character (and any other identity that pushes us to see ourselves as separate from the rest or act in isolation) is illusory and does not represent our entire personhood.

In the final section, I take the importance of others on the spiritual level one step further. First, below are some questions to consider to "live the power within" related to our connection with others.

Live the Power Within by Co-Creating with Others

— If life is a co-creation process, who are you co-creating yourself with outside of your intimate partner?

— Do you have a support group that you belong to? Is this small group of support diverse enough? How do they make up for your weaknesses?

— Do you have collaborators for your key initiatives or vocation?

— Do you have a small group of people that you can call at 3:00 AM and know they will pick up?

Living as the Divine on this Earthly Journey—Ultimate Alchemy

I am driven by the firm belief that we are Divine Beings on this Earthly journey to grow and experience our essence, which is infinite love.

Inherent to that essence is the capacity to love everyone since by nature, "infinite" includes everything. In other words, it is a part of our essence that we recognize everyone as being part of us ("oneness").

A world designed for us to experience both love and rejection

If a Higher Being wanted to create an environment on a planet where spiritual beings would experience the extremes of rejection and love, there couldn't be a better setting than Earth. Both our biology (inner wiring) and societal constructs conspire for us to have a natural tendency to love some and reject others.

Research in the developing fields of neurosociology, neuroanthropology, and neuropsychology has shown that the same neurochemicals in our brain that lead us to seek attachment to a group are the same ones that push us to reject others. (4,5)

Society preys on this natural tendency due to humans' neurochemistry, which pushes us to seek to belong. All human societies have norms, myths, and taboos that instruct their younglings to conform or become social outcasts—or, at a minimum, experience societal disapproval. The case could be made that our schools and other institutions we interact with early on (including our families) are intended to indoctrinate us to be conformists to a group or subgroup, such as religion, within the larger society. (6)

Human societies have an agenda for turning us into conformists. Cohesion within early tribes of Homo Sapiens was crucial for us defeating other homincids. An essential element of this cohesion is to promote the exclusion of outsiders. Membership in the group is more desirable because there are inclusion criteria.

Exclusion, being a tool to enable cohesion, applies to both the larger society and the subgroups within it. In most societies, there is at least one of these classes: ruling elites, religious elites, and those controlling financial resources (the Haves). This means there are at least two classes in any society: those who are part of the elites and those who are not. This is why throughout human history, there has always been discrimination against marginalized groups, as pointed out by Yuval Harari in *Sapiens* (7).

133

A world designed to push us to grow

Life on Earth is designed to push us to grow. This is, again, a biology by society interaction effect.

We come into this world as vulnerable as one could be in all aspects: physically, mentally, and spiritually. Growing physically is not optional; we are genetically pre-programmed for it. The same can also be said of our mental and spiritual development. On the latter, we don't need any individual instructions or religious teaching for this to happen. For a child born in an isolated environment (such as a tribe in the Amazon), I would posit that it's only a matter of time before they find themselves amazed by some wonder in nature that will remind them of the beauty they have inside.

Throughout history, there has always been a societal influence negatively affecting the individual's ability to grow to his or her full potential. The construct of human societies is relatively simple: in virtually all of them, there is an elite minority and then all the rest. Those in the elite class can afford a way of life or have privileges that others don't. Membership is limited, which makes it even more desirable.

In all times (and even today), most non-elites can be seen to spend so much time on survival that they cannot tend to spiritual growth. One may be tempted to argue that this was only true until the Industrial Revolution. I would make the case that even in our modern world, most workers in developed economies (and certainly in the world overall) can barely subsist on their regular income—if they have one.

The elites and those who can live comfortably are not getting off scot-free either. They worry about minding their P's (possessions, perception, or power)—growing it or protecting it—that they, too, lose track of their spiritual identity.

Ultimately, whatever social class one is in (even with little possibility for upward mobility), part of our human nature is to want to keep up with the Jones next door. Hence, the proverbial rat race amongst those living comfortably is not confined to Western or capitalistic societies.

We do get some clues about our divine origin

I mentioned earlier that nature has always been there to provide opportunities for us to be awestruck and realize that there must be some Higher Power that we are connected to, giving rise to such beauty. The other example of divine clues comes from experiencing selfless love in the form of romantic or biological (such as parent-child) relationships. Of course, this love can also happen between two friends (e.g., the poet Rumi and his mentor Shams of Tabriz, David and Jonathan in the Bible).

These loving relationships can be mirrors to our soul, reflecting for our benefit the Divine within us. At the same time, as indicated earlier, these very loving relationships can also push us away from our divine essence by excluding others outside of that relationship. The same intensity with which a mother loves a child is the same intensity with which her inner mama bear may come into play to resort to aggression to protect that child.

Outside of love and nature, the other instance where we get clues about our divine nature is through human creation. That creation can be in the form of concocting a simple recipe, an athlete making a play that calls for kinetic genius beyond explanation, or more complex ones such as pieces of music or architecture.

Why this is the ultimate alchemy

Living as the Divine (loving everyone and seeing everyone as a part of us) is the ultimate alchemy, both because of the level of challenge involved and the part of the Earthly journey.

On that, perhaps this is what the Biblical text means when it says, "I am born in sin, and my mother has conceived me in sin (Psalms 51:5)." To paraphrase, this is saying, "I came into a world where I am wired to experience separation, and generations before me have structured their society to ensure that this would happen."

A word of clarification: overcoming hate is not the main obstacle to living the Divine within. This emotion stands as such an extreme of our essence, and its raging effect on our physical body is so pronounced that it is relatively easy to see that this is an emotion we experience as we journey here on Earth. It is not our nature.

The main obstacle is indifference.

Let's think about it. We have limited capacity when it comes to building connections. Scientists have told us that we can have meaningful connections with a maximum number of 150 people (8). While most can take pride in starting this life being less self-centered than a Lone Wolf, as of the time of my writing this book, wars are happening in Darfur, in several countries in Africa that involve Muslim extremists (Boko Haram), and oppression of the Uyghurs in China. These are only the less-talked-about conflicts in our Western press. But why go that far? In America, everyone is likely living only a few zip codes away from a child who goes to school hungry for part of the year.

Regarding indifference, Jesus used an entire chapter in the Bible (Luke 15) to warn us through several parables that we cannot leave anyone untouched. This includes the parable of the lost coin (the equivalent of a penny) to tell us that we can't lose even one whom we perceive as being the smallest among us. The parable of the lost sheep also reminds us that every soul must be accounted for.

As for the parable of the prodigal son in Luke 15, I believe it should be called "the parable of the indifferent older brother." In it, Jesus tells the story of the youngest of two sons who asks for his inheritance, squanders it, and then comes back begging to be taken back by his father—even as a servant. The older brother is upset when the father throws a feast for his sibling upon his return. When the parable of the prodigal son is discussed, the focus is on the younger brother and how much love the father (G-d) has for him. What's missed is that the message was addressed to the spiritual leaders at the time, who represented the older brother in the story. The message to the older brother, who was raging against giving the younger son another chance, was, "Don't you get it? We can't afford to lose him!"

⋖⋗—⋗ ⋖—⋘

The point was made earlier that we have lived in one era as a species, which I have termed "clannism," that is, an era where part of our identity comes from belonging to a group—a nation, ethnic, religious, or social class. Several of these barriers are being dismantled. In the top 20 economies (G20) and most developed countries, birth rates are going down, leading to the inevitability that in less than a generation, majority racial groups (e.g., whites in Western countries) will become minority groups. At the same time, secularization in these countries has removed religious barriers. Even for those who still view themselves as spiritual, there is a growing ecumenical trend in which denominations set aside dogmatic differences to work together.

This is pointing to a new era that pioneers like Barbara Marx Hubbard have termed "Conscious Evolution," which refers to an era where humans join non-competing groups to co-evolve (9). The term "conscious" is in contrast to the process of biological evolution, where it happens by chance. In this era, with an agenda to create a world that benefits humanity, we will each join groups that advance that agenda based on what we feel our souls are being called to.

How do we usher in this new era?

It starts by acknowledging the Divine within us, which means recognizing that the Divine must also reside in every other human being. The next step is to become part of a group working toward a common goal that involves addressing a need—local or somewhere further out in the world. Compared to other studies, such as the Harvard study on adult development (which indicates that having quality connections with a few people promotes our well-being), what I am adding here is being part of a more structured group where participants support each other (self-realization) while at the same time working toward a common goal (which is a critical component in group dynamics to help cohesion within and can be part of the members' growth). The nature of the problem the group tackles needs to be such that it pauses some challenges. On a local level, this might take the form of being part of a group to deal with homelessness, child hunger, or economic empowerment in an area, or it might involve working on a more ambitious problem, such as building cities that are more conducive to the promotion of individuals' well-being, including their connections.

One of the issues that is dear to my heart is that of education, where we need to shift our approach from solely imparting knowledge that teaches students to earn a living toward one where we teach them to live. The type of learning I have in mind would include (at an appropriate age) exposure to tools such as enneagrams tied to the key concept of revisiting the loss of innocence. Another component of that teaching is to introduce students to several tools that can help promote spiritual growth, such as meditation. I have three personal practices that I believe any human being (including students) would benefit from—meditation, gratitude, and rest. As I have indicated before, rest isn't only about inactivity; it's about rejuvenation, which can involve activities that restore energy, creativity, and emotional well-being. These are not acts you do; for me, they are part of life. Because of my commitment to this issue, I have written an eBook that will be available for free on this book's website at https://www.watertobutter.com.

The additional practice that every college or university can incorporate right away is formally having each student become part of a cohort where they take a subset of classes together to solve a problem. This could start at the junior level, where students are less likely to transfer to another institution. As part of this cohort, students would also have to work on a joint project together, rather than taking classes together.

◄►— —►◄

Yes, this Earth will give you some heartbreaks and challenges beyond what you think you can handle. What the generations who have come before have taught us, however, is that we can solve the personal problems that come our way and create a comfortable life for ourselves and those around us.

This book is an invitation to go beyond the elemental alchemy of transforming water into butter to the ultimate alchemy, where we embark on that eternal quest of co-creating the Divine within. It is an act of co-creation that calls for us to help others co-create themselves.

Live the Power Within.

References for Chapter 10

1. Hill, N. (2009). Think and grow rich. White Dog Publishing

2. https://news.harvard.edu/gazette/story/2017/04/over-nearly-80-years-harvard-study-has-been-showing-how-to-live-a-healthy-and-happy-life/

3. https://longevity.stanford.edu/lifestyle/2023/12/18/how-social-connection-supports-longevity/

4. Raghanti MA et al. (2018). A neurochemical hypothesis for the origin of hominids. Proc Natl Acad Sci U S A. 2018 Feb 6;115(6):E1108-E1116. doi: 10.1073/pnas.1719666115. Epub 2018 Jan 22. PMID: 29358369; PMCID: PMC5819450.

5. Hare B. Survival of the Friendliest: Homo sapiens Evolved via Selection for Prosociality. Annu Rev Psychol. 2017 Jan 3;68:155-186. doi: 10.1146/annurev-psych-010416-044201. Epub 2016 Oct 12. PMID: 27732802.

6. Blackmore, S. (1999). The meme machine. Oxford University Press.

7. Harari, Y. N. (2015). Sapiens: A brief history of humankind. Harper

8. Gladwell, M. (2000). *The tipping point: How little things can make a big difference*. Little, Brown.

9. Hubbard, B. M. (1998). *Conscious evolution: Awakening the power of our social potential*. New World Library.

Made in USA - Kendallville, IN
27436_9798992064933
12.04.2024 2158